Word for Windows
at a Glance

The fastest and easiest way to learn Microsoft® Word 2.0 for Windows™

Russell A. Stultz

Wordware Publishing, Inc.
1506 Capital Avenue
Plano, Texas 75074
(214) 423-0090

Library of Congress Cataloging-in-Publication Data

Stultz, Russell Allen.
 Word 2.0 for Windows at a glance : the fastest and easiest way to
learn Microsoft Word 2.0 for Windows / Russell A. Stultz.
    p. cm.
 Includes index.
 ISBN 1-55622-348-X
 1. Microsoft Word for Windows. 2. Word processing. I. Title.
 Z52.5.M523S79 1993
 652.5'5369--dc20   93-20073
                                                               CIP

Copyright © 1993, Wordware Publishing, Inc.

All Rights Reserved

1506 Capital Avenue
Plano, Texas 75074

No part of this book may be reproduced in any form or by any means without permission in writing from Wordware Publishing, Inc.

Printed in the United States of America

ISBN 1-55622-348-X
10 9 8 7 6 5 4 3 2 1
9304

All inquiries for volume purchases of this book should be addressed to Wordware Publishing, Inc., at the above address. Telephone inquiries may be made by calling:
(214) 423-0090

Contents

1—About This Book 1
2—Terms, Definitions, and Conventions..2
3—Menus and Dialog Boxes 4
4—Toolbar and Ribbon..6
5—Ruler, Status Line, Scroll Bars...8
6—Opening Files..10
7—Closing Files 12
8—Saving and Naming Documents 14
9—Moving Around in a Document 16
10—Changing Document Views; Hidden Characters..18
11—Inserting and Deleting Text 20
12—Selecting, Cutting, Copying, and Pasting Text 22
13—Undo and Repeat Operations 24
14—Working with Styles...26
15—Fonts, Type Sizes, and Text Attributes (bold, italic, underline) 28
16—Margins, Indents, Outdents, and Line Spacing 30
17—Setting Tabs 32
18—Formatting Text—Part 1 (Pages, Paragraphs, and Characters) 34
19—Formatting Text—Part 2 (Sections) 36
20—Numbered and Bulleted Lists 38
21—Find and Replace 40
22—Working with Tables—Part 1 (Table Creation) 42
23—Working with Tables—Part 2 (Table Editing) 44
24—Working with Columns..46
25—Working with Frames; Runarounds 48
26—Adding Borders and Lines 50
27—Headers and Footers 52
28—Footnotes and Annotations 54
29—Page Numbers and Dates 56
30—Bookmarks (Finding Your Place)...58
31—Inserting Special Characters and Symbols 60

Contents (continued)

- 32—Dot Leaders ... 62
- 33—Indexes and Tables of Contents ... 64
- 34—Spelling Checks ... 66
- 35—Grammar Checks ... 68
- 36—Using the Thesaurus ... 70
- 37—Using Hyphenation ... 72
- 38—Opening Multiple Documents with the Window Menu ... 74
- 39—Automating Your Work with Macros ... 76
- 40—Print Preview ... 78
- 41—Printing Operations—Part 1 ... 80
- 42—Printing Operations—Part 2 ... 82
- 43—Working with Graphs—Part 1 ... 84
- 44—Working with Graphs—Part 2 ... 86
- 45—Working with Drawings—Part 1 ... 88
- 46—Working with Drawings—Part 2 ... 90
- 47—Working with Equations—Part 1 ... 92
- 48—Working with Equations—Part 2 ... 94
- 49—Print Merge—Part 1 ... 96
- 50—Print Merge—Part 2 ... 98
- 51—Fancy Type with MS WordArt—Part 1 ... 100
- 52—Fancy Type with MS WordArt—Part 2 ... 102
- 53—Finding and Working with Files ... 104
- 54—Exchanging Files with Other Programs ... 106

- Appendix A—Shortcut Keys ... 109
- Appendix B—Field Codes ... 113
- Alphabetical Index ... 115

Section 1—About This Book

INTRODUCTION

This book gives you instant access to the features of Microsoft® Word 2.0 for Windows. You can think of it as an instant graphical reference/tutorial. It is filled with keyed illustrations of document examples. Each illustrated example has a corresponding, easy-to-follow procedure that guides you through the steps necessary to accomplish the desired effect. A rich array of Word features is provided. You'll find everything from simple editing operations to the creation and use of tables, multicolumn text, numbered lists, footnotes, graphs, pictures, equations, macros, and much more.

HOW TO USE THIS BOOK

You can access information quickly using the Contents listing at the front of the book or the alphabetical index at the rear of the book. For example, if you wish to create a table, you can look up Working with Tables in the contents or simply "Tables" in the alphabetical index. Turn to the pages that show examples of tables. Find a table that is similar to the one you want to create and read the creation instructions on the adjacent page. The entire process only takes a few minutes. You can learn any Word 2.0 operation in record time using this book.

HARDWARE AND SOFTWARE REQUIREMENTS

Your hardware should be equipped to run Microsoft Windows 3.0 or 3.1 (3.1 is recommended). This requires MS-DOS 3.3 to 6.0, a minimum of two megabytes of random-access memory (more is better), EGA or VGA graphics, and hard disk and floppy disk drives. Your computer should also be equipped with a mouse. Both Microsoft Windows and Microsoft Word 2.0 should be installed on your computer and ready to run.

WHAT YOU SHOULD KNOW

You should be familiar with common DOS commands, such as COPY and FORMAT, and the operation of Microsoft Windows. You should also know how to use a mouse and your keyboard. If you wish to obtain information on MS-DOS and Windows, consider the following books from Wordware Publishing, Inc.

> *Illustrated MS-DOS 5.0*
> *Illustrated Windows 3.1*
> *Learn DOS in a Day*
> *Learn Windows in a Day*

Now turn to Section 2 where terminology and conventions used in this book are presented.

2 Section 2—Terms, Definitions, and Conventions

INTRODUCTION

This section defines some common terminology and conventions used in this book. Once you've browsed this information, you should understand the descriptive recipes that tell you how to perform the many Word operations presented in this book.

TERMS AND DEFINITIONS

The following terms are used in this book. Many of the items defined are illustrated in the next three sections of this book. Familiarize yourself with these so you will have a clear understanding of the term when encountered in a procedure or on an illustration.

Button (or *Action* Button)—A rectangular selection button, such as an **OK**, **Yes**, **No**, or **Cancel** button. Performs an action when clicked. When a button is highlighted (or boldface), it is activated when the Enter key is pressed.

Check Box—A box in which an "X" is placed to set the way Word operates.

Ellipsis—Three dots following a menu entry to indicate further user dialog. When no ellipsis is present, selecting a menu item performs the indicated action.

Default—A predetermined setting which is automatically used unless overridden by an alternate user selection.

Dialog Box—A box that is used to set the way a Word operation works; typically includes text boxes, option buttons, check boxes, and action buttons.

Icon—A displayed symbol that performs an operation when clicked with the mouse pointer.

Keystroke—A typed or pressed key.

Menu—A list of displayed selections.

Menu Bar—A row of menu names at the top of the screen.

Mouse Pointer—An arrow or cross hair that designates the mouse position on the screen.

Option (or *Radio*) Button—A round button within a dialog box, such as those displayed in the Insert|Page Numbers dialog box. An interior black dot indicates selection; only one option button at a time can be on.

Ribbon—A horizontal set of selection boxes and icons used to set document styles, fonts, type sizes, text styles (bold, italic, underline), text alignment, tab types, and the display of hidden symbols.

Scroll Bar—Located at the left or bottom of the screen; used to adjust the page display position on the screen.

Text Box—A box within which text or numbers are typed. For example, text boxes are used to type or select a paragraph style name or type size (in points).

Toolbar—A horizontal row of icons; each icon performs a Word operation.

Section 2—Terms, Definitions, and Conventions

CONVENTION USED IN THIS BOOK

Boldfaced key names and text strings exist in the procedures found in this book. Boldfaced characters tell you that the indicated keys are pressed or typed. If a + sign connects keys, they are pressed and released together. If separated by commas, each key is pressed independently. A few examples are provided to clarify these conventions. In addition, mouse operations and screen objects, such as buttons, are also described.

Alt+F—Press and hold Alt, type F, and then release Alt.

Alt, F, A—Press and release Alt, type F, and then type A.

Enter—Press the Enter key.

Ctrl+I—Press and hold Ctrl, type I, and then release Ctrl.

Click—Press and release the left mouse button. (The right mouse button is sometimes used to select a column within a table or columnar area of text.)

Drag—Press and hold the left mouse button down, drag the mouse pointer to a designated location, and release the left mouse button.

Pick—Pick a designated item with the mouse pointer.

Select—Pick a passage of text, an item in a menu, an icon, a checkbox, or an option button.

Highlight—Select a character or an entire passage of text so that it is displayed in inverse video (or "highlighted"). You can hold the Shift key down while picking a passage with selection keys including your mouse, arrow keys, End, etc. Select an entire document with Ctrl+NumPad 5.

Section 3—Menus and Dialog Boxes

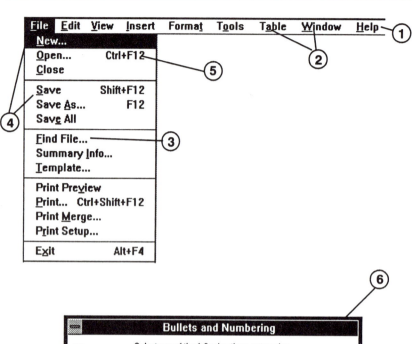

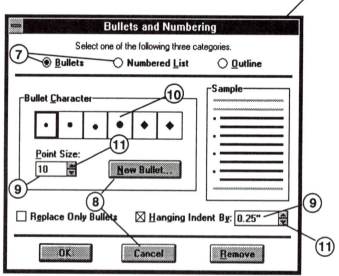

Section 3—Menus and Dialog Boxes

Key	Description	Procedure or Definition
1	Menu bar	Click a menu name with your mouse or press **Alt+x**, where x is the underlined letter (or *key assignment*) within a menu name.
2	Menu name	When clicked with mouse or when **Alt+x** is pressed, where *x* is an underlined letter, a list of selections is displayed in a pull-down menu.
3	Menu selection	An entry within a pull-down menu; activated when picked with a mouse or selected with the key assignment (underlined letter). An ellipsis (...) indicates a following dialog box.
4	Key assignment	A key (such as a function key, key sequence, or underlined letter within a menu name) that is used to start an operation or display a dialog box.
5	Shortcut key	A key sequence that provides direct access to a Word operation without having to go through a series of menu selections.
6	Dialog box	A box that displays user choices that correspond to some word processing or formatting operation.
7	Option buttons	An option button is active, or "turned on," when filled.
8	Action button	A rectangular button used to perform an indicated operation, such as **OK**, **Cancel**, etc.
9	Text box	A text entry box that accepts supplied values from the keyboard.
10	Selection box	A group of displayed graphic representations from which you can set up an operation by selecting the desired graphic.
11	Increase/Decrease selector	Used to increase (up arrow) or decrease (down arrow) a corresponding value, such as margins, tab stops, and spacing.

6 Section 4—The Toolbar and Ribbon

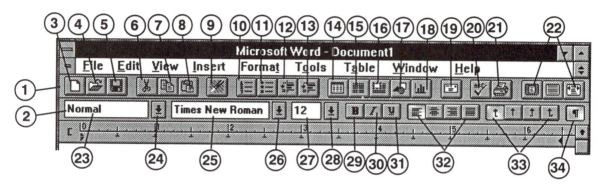

Key	Description	Procedure or Definition
1	Toolbar	A series of icons that provide quick access to a Word operation, such as file handling, editing, and formatting operations. You can also use a corresponding menu selection to accomplish the same result.
2	Ribbon	A group of text boxes and formatting icons used to set text styles, fonts, type sizes, character attributes (bold, italic, or underline), text alignment (left, center, flush right, justified), tab types (left, center, right, decimal), and hidden character display.
3	New document icon	Click to open new document (same as the **File|New** menu selection).
4	File folder icon	Click to display a list of files (**File|Open**).
5	Diskette icon	Click to save the active file (**File|Save**).
6	Scissor icon	Click to cut a selected (highlighted) passage to the *clipboard* (memory buffer from which selections are *pasted*) (**Edit|Cut** or **Ctrl+X**).
7	Copy icon	Click to copy selected passage to clipboard (**Edit|Copy** or **Ctrl+C**).
8	Paste icon	Click to paste previously cut passage (**Edit|Paste** or **Ctrl+V**).
9	Eraser icon	Click to undo last operation (**Ctrl+Z**).
10	Numbered list icon	Click to convert selected paragraphs to a numbered list (set format with Tools|Bullets and Numbering).
11	Bulleted list icon	Click to convert selected paragraphs to a bulleted list (set format with Tools|Bullets and Numbering).
12	Outdent icon	Click to outdent one tab stop. This shifts the left margin or the current paragraph to the left by one tab stop (**Ctrl+M**).
13	Indent icon	Click to indent the left margin of the current paragraph one tab stop to the right (**Ctrl+N**).

Section 4—The Toolbar and Ribbon

Key	Description	Procedure or Definition
14	Table icon	Click to convert a selected passage of tabular text to a table (**Table|Insert Table**).
15	Column icon	Click to convert selected section to multicolumn text (**Format|Columns**).
16	Frame icon	Click to place selected passage or illustration in a frame or to create an empty frame (**Insert|Frame**).
17	Draw icon	Click to start Microsoft Draw program. Commonly used to create or edit a drawing and insert it into a document.
18	Graph icon	Click to start Microsoft Graph program. Commonly used to create or edit a graph and insert it into a document.
19	Envelope icon	Click to print an address on an envelope. If the current document is a letter, Word "finds" the address. You can also type an address in a displayed dialog box or highlight it on the current document.
20	Spell check icon	Click to check the spelling of the current document or a selected word or passage.
21	Printer icon	Click to print a single copy of the current document.
22	Page display icons (3)	Click to change the way a document is displayed (**View|Zoom**).
23	Style box	Pick to select text style (**Format|Style** or **Ctrl+S**).
24	Style box pick list	Pick to display a list of available style formats.
25	Font box	Pick to select an available font (**Format|Character** or **Ctrl+F**).
26	Font box pick list	Pick to display a list of available type fonts.
27	Type size icon	Pick to select a desired type size (the default is 10).
28	Type size pick list	Pick to display a list of available type sizes that correspond to the selected font.
29	Boldface icon	Pick to set text to boldface (**Ctrl+B**) or set boldface text to normal.
30	Italic icon	Pick to set text to italic (**Ctrl+I**) or to set italic text to normal.
31	Underline icon	Pick to set text to underline (**Ctrl+U**) or to set underlined text to normal.
32	Text alignment icons (4)	Pick appropriate icon to set text flush left (**Ctrl+L**), centered (**Ctrl+E**), flush right (**Ctrl+R**), or right-hand justified (**Ctrl+J**).
33	Tab style icons	Pick to set tab stop settings to flush left (the default style), centered, flush right, or decimal aligned.
34	Paragraph icon	Pick to turn the display of hidden characters (tabs, paragraphs, spaces, etc.) on or off.

8 Section 5—Ruler, Scroll Bars, and Status Line

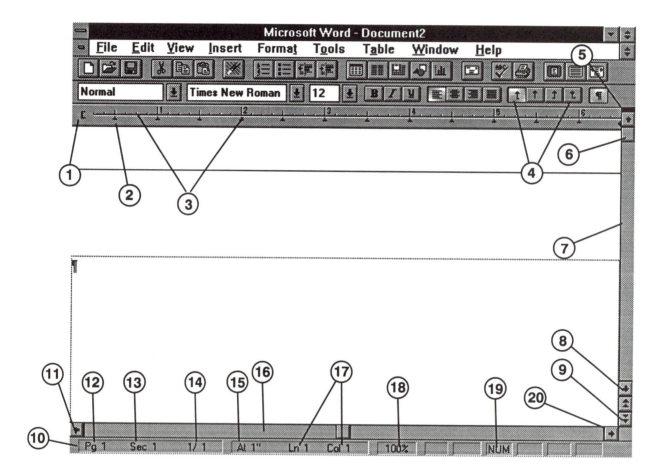

Section 5—Ruler, Scroll Bars, and Status Line

Key	Description	Procedure or Definition
1	Ruler	Displays current margin, tab, and indent settings.
2	Default tab stop	The inverted "T" represents a default tab setting, as specified using the **Format|Tabs** dialog box.
3	Ruler scale	A horizontal scale graduated in eighth inches; indicates the page width and position of margins, tab stops, and indents.
4	Tab style icons	Pick to select a tab stop style; position the tab at the selected location on ruler. Drag down and off the ruler to remove a tab setting or use the **Format|Tabs** dialog box.
5	Scroll up arrow	Move up (or toward the top) of the document. Picking above the scroll up arrow displays a split double arrow. Drag down to split the page into two "panes." Drag back to the top to remove the split.
6	Vertical scroll button	Drag up or down to move the page display up or down.
7	Vertical scroll bar	Shows vertical position of display relative to entire document.
8	Scroll down arrow	Move down (or toward the bottom) of the document.
9	Next/Previous page icons	Move to the next (down arrow) or previous (up arrow) page.
10	Status line	Displays information about the document including page, section, line, and column numbers, zoom percentage, Num Lock status, and typeover or insert mode. (OVR is displayed when in typeover mode.)
11	Scroll left arrow	Move the page display from right to left.
12	Current page number	The number of the current page; when **F5** is pressed, you are prompted to type a page number here. When **Tools|Calculate** is used to find the sum of a selected series of numbers, the answer is displayed here.
13	Section number	Sections are used to permit multiple formats within a document. For example, Section 1 can be two column with indents at 1.25 inches while Section 2 can be three column with indents at 1 inch.
14	Page number/total number of pages	This notation shows the current page number and the total number of pages in the current document.
15	Vertical position	The current cursor position relative to the top of the page.
16	Horizontal scroll bar	Shows horizontal position of display relative to total page width.
17	Line and column no.	The current cursor position expressed as a line and column number.
18	Zoom percentage	The displayed width expressed as a percent. Use the **View|Zoom** dialog box or page display icons to change the width of the display.
19	Num Lock status	The current status of the Num Lock key; NUM is displayed when on.
20	Scroll right arrow	Move page display from left to right.

Section 6—Opening Files

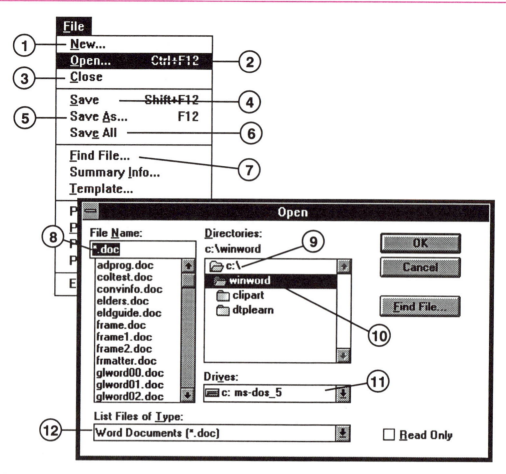

Key	Description	Procedure or Definition
	General	When you start Word a blank page is displayed; Word gives the first blank document the name *Document1*. Word names the second "new" document *Document2*, and so on. Create a new document by typing and saving it (see Section 7) or open an existing document. The most recently saved document names are displayed at the bottom of the **File** menu. You can open one of these by clicking a name with the mouse or typing the indicated number when the **File** menu is displayed.
1	New...	Use this **File** menu selection or the leftmost page icon on the toolbar to open a new document.
2	Open...	Use this selection, click the file folder icon, or press **Ctrl+F12** to open an existing file. The **Open** dialog box is used to select the document (see items 8 through 12 below).

Section 6—Opening Files

Key	Description	Procedure or Definition
3	Close	Use this selection to close the currently open file. You are automatically prompted to save the file before closing if changes have been made.
4	Save	Use this selection or the diskette icon on the toolbar to save the current document. If not previously saved, you are prompted for a file name.
5	Save As...	Use this selection or press **Shift+F12** to save the current document under a new file name. The **Save As** dialog box prompts you to enter a new file name.
6	Save All	Use this selection to save all open files. You can see a list of the open files at the bottom of the **Window** menu.
7	Find File...	Use this selection to locate and preview files using the **Find File** dialog box. The Options button lets you view title, summary info, content, or statistics. You can also use the **Find File** dialog box to open, copy, delete, and print one or multiple files. To print multiple files, press **Ctrl** and pick the desired file names so they are highlighted. Then click the **Print** button.
8	File Name box	Type the name of the file you want to open or select the file from the pick list. You can type ***.*** to display all files; type ***.ltr** to see all files having the extension ltr, etc. (See item 12 below.)
9	Directories box	Double click here or highlight and press **Enter** to select the root directory of the currently logged disk drive. Double clicking C:\ takes you to the root directory and displays a list of all subdirectories that are subordinate to the root.
10	Subdirectory (or File Path) box	Double click the desired directory name to see a list of the corresponding files.
11	Drives selection box	Click the down arrow to display a list of disk drives. Pick the desired disk drive from the list. Double click or highlight and press **Enter**.
12	List Files of Type box	Click the down arrow to display a list of common file types including *.*. (The normal file type is *.doc.) The selected type is used in the File Name box. You can also type the file type directly into the File Name box.

12 **Section 7—Closing Files**

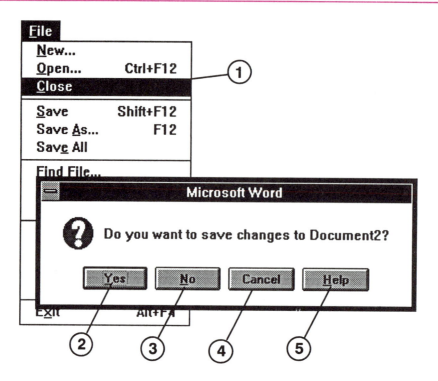

Section 7—Closing Files

Key	Description	Procedure or Definition
1	File|Close	Pick **File|Close** to close the current document. Note that Word for Windows assigns the temporary name Document1, Document2, etc. to a new, unsaved document.
2	Yes button	If the document is new or changed, a dialog box is displayed. Pick Yes to save the document; if unamed, the **Save As** dialog box is displayed (see Section 8).
3	No button	Pick No to discard the document or changes.
4	Cancel button	Pick Cancel to return to the current document.
5	Help button	Pick Help to review information about the close operation.

14 Section 8—Saving and Naming Documents

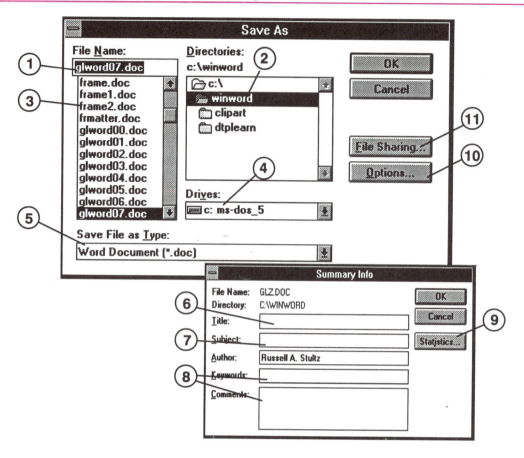

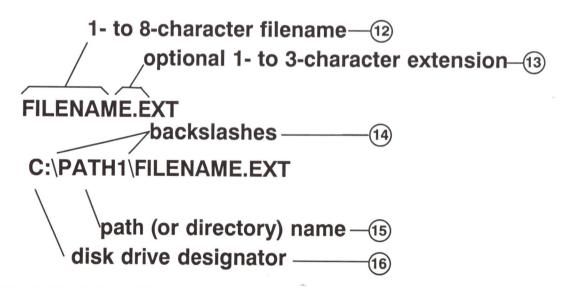

Section 8—Saving and Naming Documents 15

Key	Description	Procedure or Definition
	General (See the File menu items 3 thru 7 in Section 6.)	Use **File|Save As** (or press **F12**) to give a displayed document a new name before saving it. Use Save (or the disk icon on the toolbar) to save changes to an existing file to disk. Word prompts you for a file name when creating and saving the default *Document1* file.
1	File Name box	Type a file name here and click **OK** or press **Enter** to save. See items 12 through 16 for information about file names, paths, and disk drives.
2	Directories box	Pick a directory here (or highlight and press **Enter**).
3	File Name pick list	You can pick an existing file name if you want to replace it with the current document.
4	Drives box	Press the down arrow to display and pick a different disk drive.
5	Save File as Type box	Use this box to save the current document in a different file format.
6	Title box	When using Summary Info, type a descriptive document title here. (Summary Info is suppressed by unmarking the "Prompt for Summary Info" check box in the Tools|Options|Save dialog box.)
7	Subject box	Type a brief description of the subject here.
8	Keywords/Comments box	Use these areas to type additional information about the document.
9	Statistics button	Click to display information including file name, creation date, editing time, file size, and more.
10	Options button	Click to set Save As options: create backup document, prompt for summary info, periodic auto save, and allow "fast save."
11	File Sharing button	Click this button if you want to establish a document password. You can permit others to add annotations but prevent them from making changes.
12	File name	A 1- to 8-character file name consisting of letters or numbers; should be descriptive to identify the contents of the file.
13	File extension	File extensions are optional. They may be from 1 to 3 characters. Extensions are typically used to identify the file type. EXE and COM designate program files; DOC and TXT designate document and text files, etc.
14	Backslashes	Backslashes are used to separate path names from disk drive designators and file names.
15	Path (or directory) name	The file path in which a file is located. File paths are used to organize files into separate disk directories. A complete file name includes the disk drive designator, path name, file name, and extension. You can omit the disk drive and path name when a file is in the current directory.
16	Disk drive designator	The disk drive on which a file is located. Disk drives A and B are removable drives; C and higher designate hard (fixed) and memory (RAM) drives and tape devices. Drive letters always include a colon.

Section 9—Moving Around in a Document

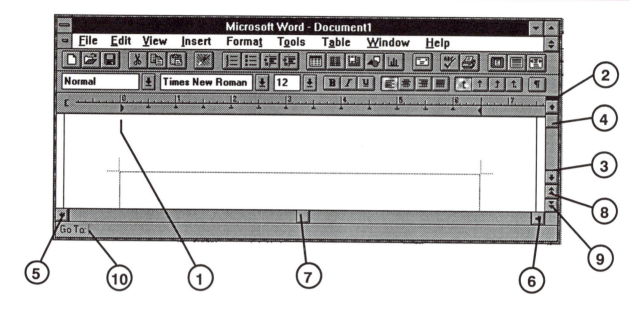

Section 9—Moving Around in a Document

Key	Description	Procedure or Definition
	General	**Special Cursor Control Keys:** Right/Left Arrow—Move one character left or right. Ctrl+Right Arrow—Move one word right. Ctrl+Left Arrow—Move one word left. Home—Go to the beginning of the current line. End—Go to the end of the current line. Ctrl+Home—Go to the beginning of the document. Ctrl+End—Go to the end of the document. Alt+Home—Go to the beginning of the first column (in a table). Alt+End—Go to beginning of last column (in a table). Ctrl+PgUp—Go to top of current screen display. Ctrl+PgDn—Go to bottom of current screen display. Alt+PgUp—Go to the top of the column (in a table). Alt+PgDn—Go to the bottom of the column (in a table). Ctrl+Enter—Insert page break; then move to the top of the next page.
1	Text cursor	The editing point within the current document.
2	Scroll up	Click with the mouse pointer to scroll the document up.
3	Scroll down	Click with the mouse pointer to scroll the document down.
4	Drag up/down	Drag up or down with the mouse pointer to move the document vertically.
5	Scroll right	Click with the mouse pointer to scroll the document left to right.
6	Scroll left	Click with the mouse pointer to scroll the document right to left.
7	Drag left/right	Drag left or right with the mouse pointer to move the document horizontally.
8	Previous page	Click with the mouse to move to the previous page.
9	Next page	Click with the mouse to move to the next page.
10	Go To: (F5)	Press **F5**, type a valid document page number, and press **Enter**.

Section 10—Changing Document Views; Hidden Characters

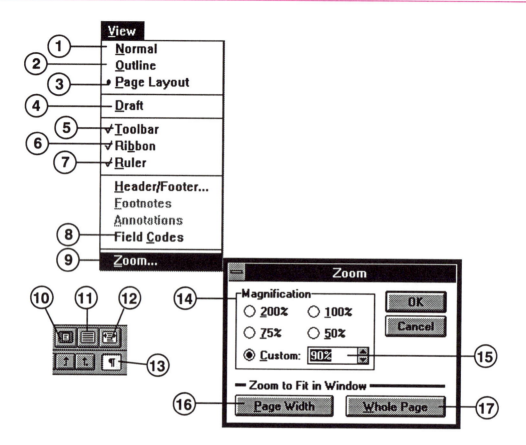

Section 10—Changing Document Views; Hidden Characters

Key	Description	Procedure or Definition
1	View|Normal	The default mode, which is the preferred text entry and editing mode.
2	View|Outline	Pick to display a document in outline mode (showing paragraph subordination).
3	View|Page Layout	Pick to display a document in WYSIWYG (*what you see is what you get*) mode.
4	View|Draft	Pick to display a document in draft mode.
5	View|Toolbar	Pick to display or hide the toolbar (shortcut icons).
6	View|Ribbon	Pick to display or hide the ribbon (used to select the style, font, point size, text attributes, text alignment, etc.).
7	View|Ruler	Pick to display or hide the ruler above the document (showing tab and margin settings).
8	View|Field Codes	Pick to display special field codes for page numbers, dates, etc. Field codes are inside braces. (See Appendix B.)
9	View|Zoom	Pick to display the **Zoom** dialog box which is used to modify the display size of the current document.
10	Whole page icon	Pick to display a whole-page view (a shortcut alternative to **View|Zoom** to Whole Page—item 17 below).
11	Page width icon	Pick to display a page-wide view (a shortcut alternative to **View|Zoom** to Page Width—item 16 below).
12	Zoom 100% icon	Pick to display a full-page (100%) normal document view (a shortcut alternative to **View|Zoom** to Magification 100%).
13	Paragraph icon	Pick to display or hide special symbols that designate such entries as carriage returns (¶), tabs (→), space characters (·), and table cell delimiters.
14	Zoom|Magnification	Pick a magnification that best suits your display needs; custom zooms are also available by entering a zoom value in the Custom box.
15	Custom zoom value	Enter a value, such as 88 for 88 percent of a full-page (100%) view.
16	Zoom to Page Width	Pick this button to display a document from margin to margin.
17	Zoom to Whole Page	Pick this button to display a miniature view of an entire page.

Section 11—Inserting and Deleting Text

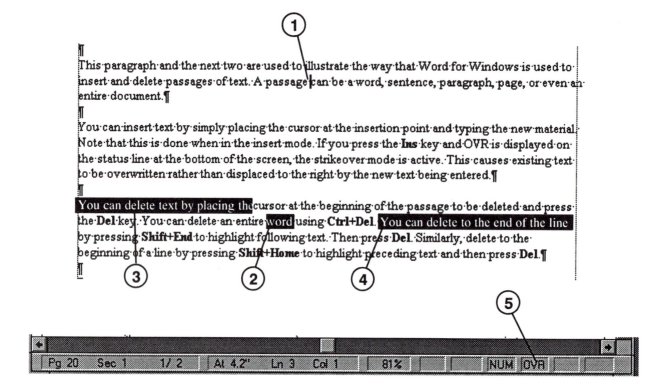

Section 11—Inserting and Deleting Text

Key	Description	Procedure or Definition
	General	You can cut or copy text and graphics to the "clipboard." Once on the clipboard, use paste to insert the material from the clipboard to the current cursor position. See Section 12 for more information about cut, copy, and paste. Use the following procedures for routine insert and delete operations.
	Deleting a graphic	Select the graphic (picture or frame) by clicking in it with your mouse so that *handles* are displayed. (Handles are solid squares located at the corners and center points of the surrounding frame.) Then press **Del** to delete the graphic from the document.
1	Insertion point (cursor)	Position the cursor to the point within a document at which text is to be inserted (use the arrow keys or mouse). Insert new text by typing it. Following text moves to the right and down as inserted text is entered. **Note:** You cannot insert text if OVR is displayed on the status line at the bottom of the screen (see 5 below).
2	Delete character or word	Position the cursor at the beginning of the character or word. Press **Del** to delete a single character at a time. Press **Ctrl+Del** to delete an entire word at a time.
3	Delete to the beginning of the current line	Position the cursor following the text to be deleted. Press **Shift+Home** to highlight all text to the beginning of the line. Press **Del** to delete the selected text.
4	Delete to the end of the current line	Position the cursor in front of the text to be deleted. Press **Shift+End** to highlight all text to the end of the line. Press **Del** to delete the selected text.
5	Insert/Strikeover mode	Press **Ins** to alternate between the insert and strikeover mode. OVR is displayed on the status line at the bottom of the screen when the strikeover mode is active. Otherwise, the insert mode is active; the insert mode is the normal (or *default*) setting.

22 Section 12—Selecting, Cutting, Pasting, and Copying

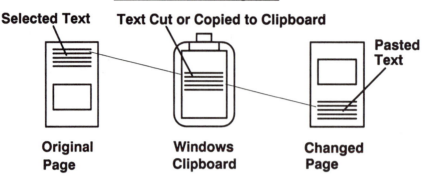

Cut & Paste Diagram

① Text is selected by either dragging it with the mouse or using the Arrow keys while holding down the Shift key. Graphic objects are selected by clicking on them to display the handles. Once selected, you can *cut* the text from the document using Edit|Cut or by pressing **Ctrl+X**. When cut, the selected text or graphic is put on the Windows clipboard.

You can also copy selected text or graphic objects. This leaves it in its original location and, like cut, also places it on the clipboard. Use Edit|Copy or press **Ctrl+C** to perform the copy operation. Once on the clipboard, text, graphics, or both (if both were selected and cut or copied at the same time) can be pasted at the cursor position.

To paste, place the cursor at the insertion (or *paste*) point. Then use Edit|Paste or press **Ctrl+V** to paste the contents of the clipboard in the document.

② Text is selected by either dragging it with the mouse or using the Arrow keys while holding down the Shift key.

③ Graphic objects are selected by clicking on them to display the handles. Once selected, you can *cut* the text from the document using Edit|Cut or by pressing **Ctrl+X**. When cut, the selected text or graphic is put on the Windows clipboard.

Section 12—Selecting, Cutting, Pasting, and Copying   23

Key	Description	Procedure or Definition
1	Selected text	Select text by dragging it with the mouse or by holding the **Shift** key down while moving through it using a cursor (arrow) key. **Selection Tips:** Use the following procedures to select large passages of text. Select entire document—Use **Edit|Select All** or press **Ctrl+NumPad 5**. Select entire table—Position cursor in table. Use **Table|Select Table** or press **Alt+NumPad 5**. Select rest of line—Press **Shift+End**. Select to beginning of line—Press **Shift+Home**. Select to end of document—Press **Ctrl+Shift+End**. Select to beginning of document—Press **Ctrl+Shift+Home**. Select entire line in text or table—Move cursor to left margin until hollow arrow symbol is displayed. Click left mouse button. Select single cell in table—Move cursor to left edge of cell until hollow arrow symbol is displayed. Click left mouse buttton. Select single column in table—Move cursor to top of column until solid arrow points down. Click right mouse button.
2	Copied and pasted text	The boxed text was cut (using **Edit|Cut**, the Scissor icon, or **Ctrl+X**). Next, it was pasted by positioning the cursor at the insertion point and using either **Edit|Paste**, the Clipboard icon, or by pressing **Ctrl+V**.
3	Cut text	This paragraph is identical to the first one, except the first sentence was removed by selecting and cutting it from the paragraph.

Section 13—Undo and Repeat Operations

① **Edit**
Undo Typing   Ctrl+Z
③ **Repeat Typing**   F4

Cu̱t   Ctrl+X
Copy   Ctrl+C
Paste   Ctrl+V
Paste Special...
Select All   Ctrl+NumPad 5

Find...
Replace...
Go To...   F5
Glossary...

Links...
Object...

② This is a new era of technology.
This is a new era of technology.
This is a new era of technology.
④ This is a new era of technology.
This is a new era of technology.
This is a new era of technology.

⑥ **Edit**
Undo Edit Clear   Ctrl+Z
⑦ **Repeat Edit Clear**   F4

Cu̱t   Ctrl+X
Copy   Ctrl+C
Paste   Ctrl+V
Paste Special...
Select All   Ctrl+NumPad 5

Find...
Replace...
Go To...   F5
Glossary...

Links...
Object...

This is a new era of technology.
This is a new era of technology ⑤
This is a new era of technology
This is a new era of technology

Section 13—Undo and Repeat Operations 25

Key	Description	Procedure or Definition
	General	Editing and formatting operations and the last typed passage can be undone using **Edit|Undo** (or you can either click the Eraser icon on the toolbar or use the **Ctrl+Z** shortcut key). Similarly, editing, formatting, and typed passages can be repeated using **Edit|Repeat** *item* (or **F4**), where the last operation performed (like "Typing" or "Edit Clear") is displayed in place of *item*.
1	Undo Typing	To undo the last passage of text you typed, use **Edit|Undo Typing**. You may want to use the Eraser icon (or press **Ctrl+Z**) to achieve the same result.
2	Repeating Text	Type a passage to be repeated. The example shows the line "This is a new era of technology." The **Enter** key is pressed at the end of the line.
3	Repeat Typing	Use **Edit|Repeat Typing** (or press **F4**) for each text repetition you want. **Tips**—If the text was cut rather than deleted, the Edit menu displays "Undo Cut" and "Repeat Cut." Similarly, when a Paste operation is performed, the Edit menu displays "Undo Paste" and "Repeat Paste." Word also knows when a page break is inserted as the Edit menu displays "Undo Insert Page Break."
4	Repeated text	**Repeat Typing** was used five times to produce the result shown in the example.
5	Deleted text	The example text was selected and then deleted using the **Del** key (the text could have been cut also).
6	Undo Edit Clear	After a deletion, you can undo it using **Edit|Undo Edit Clear** (or by pressing **Ctrl+Z**). The selected text reappears as shown in item 5 in the example.
7	Repeat Edit Clear	Use the **Edit|Repeat...** (or **F4**) selection to repeat the last editing or formatting operation.

Section 14—Working with Styles

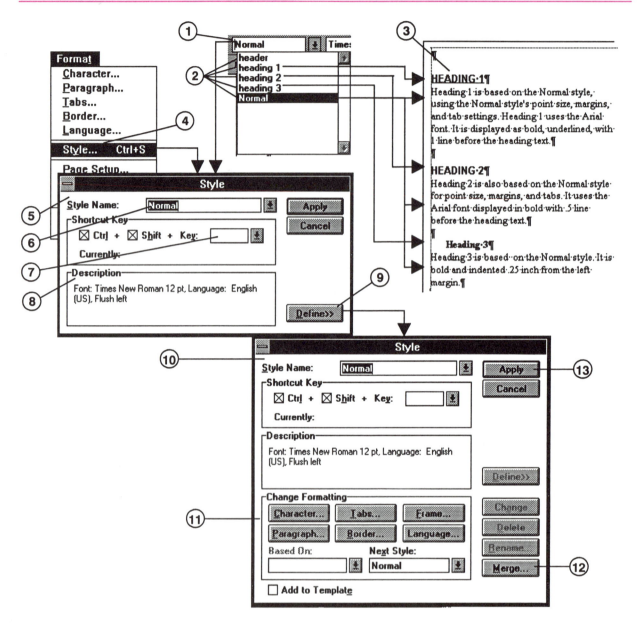

Section 14—Working with Styles

Key	Description	Procedure or Definition
	General	Styles are assigned to paragraphs of text by placing the cursor within the paragraph or line of text and selecting a style name from the pull-down box on the ribbon. The applied style name is displayed in the style box. The default style (the one delivered with Word) is called Normal. You can modify and create new styles. To modify the Normal style, open the NORMAL.DOT document, change the font, point size, page setup, etc., and then save it. New styles can be created by assigning the style attributes to your text, entering the style box, and typing a new style name of your choosing. Styles can be embedded in the current document or be global (available to all documents).
1	Current style name	The name of the style at the cursor position is displayed in the style name box on the ribbon. "Normal" is shown in the example.
2	Available style names	Clicking the down arrow next to the style name box displays a list of available style names.
3	Different styles shown	Heading 1, heading 2, heading 3, and the Normal styles are pictured.
4	Format|Style menu	Pick **Format|Style** (or **Ctrl+S** twice) to display the **Style** dialog box.
5	Style dialog box	Use to assign a shortcut key, to view current settings, to add a new style, or to change the format of an existing style.
6	Style Name box	Use to select an available style or to type the name of a new style.
7	Shortcut Key box	Use to assign a **Ctrl+Shift+x** shortcut key sequence to the displayed style. You can substitute A-Z, 0-9, F2-F12, Ins, and Del for x.
8	Description	A description of the selected style is displayed here.
9	Define button	Pick Define to access Word's Change Formatting selections.
10	Define style	Provides access to style formatting operations.
11	Change Formatting	Use Character for font, size, spacing, etc.; use Paragraph for alignment, indentation, spacing, etc.; use Tabs for tab settings; use Border to apply a border; use Frame to add or remove a frame and to specify frame settings; use Language and pick one to create a multilingual document. Enter an existing style name in the Based On box if you wish to use format settings of the named style. The style name in the Next Style box automatically follows the style being defined.
12	Other style buttons	Use Merge to extract style settings either from or to another document (or *template*). Use Change to modify the style; use Delete to remove the style; use Rename to change the name of the style.
13	Apply button	Applies the style settings; similar to an OK button.

Section 15—Fonts, Type Sizes, and Text Attributes (Bold, Italic, Underline)

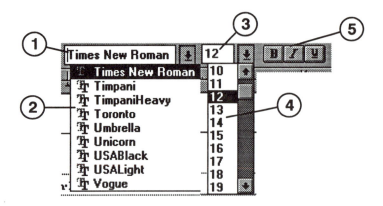

Section 15—Fonts, Type Sizes, and Text Attributes (Bold, Italic, Underline)

Key	Description	Procedure or Definition
	General	Picking a font name, point size, and/or text attribute (bold, italic, or underscore) applies it to selected text or to text that is entered immediately following the selection.
1	Font name box	The name of the font in use is displayed in this box on the ribbon. You can select the box with your mouse or by pressing **Ctrl+F**, type a valid font name, or pick one from the list that is displayed when you press the Down Arrow. Pressing **Ctrl+F** twice displays the **Format|Character** dialog box, where additional text attributes are selected.
2	Font name pick list	View available font names by putting the cursor in the font name box and either pick the down arrow symbol or pressing the Down Arrow key. An icon to the left of the font name designates the font type; TT indicates a True Type font.
3	Point size box	The name of the point size in use is displayed in this box on the ribbon. You can select the box with your mouse, type a new value, or pick one from the list of numbers that is displayed when you press the Down Arrow. <u>Shortcut Keys:</u> **Ctrl+F2** increases selected text by 1 point; **Ctrl+Shift+F2** decreases selected text by 1 point.
4	Point size pick list	View available type sizes by putting the cursor in the type size box and either pick the down arrow symbol or press the Down Arrow key.
5	Text attribute icons	Pick one or more text attribute icons to apply boldface, italic, or underline to selected text or text that is entered immediately following the selection. <u>Shortcut Keys:</u> **Ctrl+B** = boldface, **Ctrl+I** = italic, **Ctrl+U** = underline.
6	Font examples	Several font styles, sizes, and attributes are used in the list of examples. You can experiment with fonts, sizes, and attributes to achieve a satisfactory result.

30 Section 16—Margins, Indents, Outdents, and Line Spacing

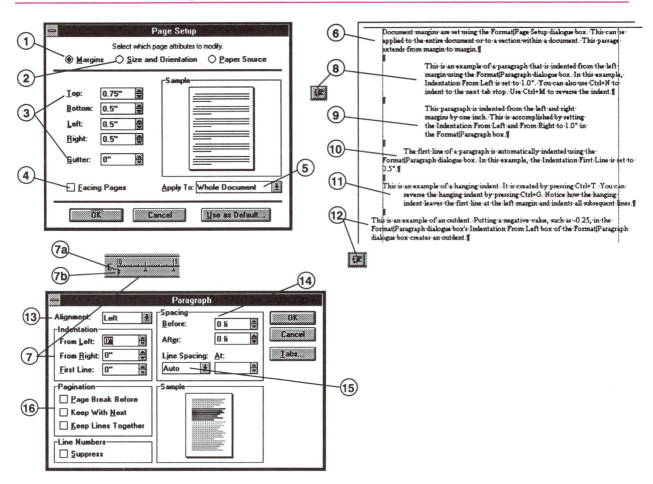

Section 16—Margins, Indents, Outdents, and Line Spacing

Key	Description	Procedure or Definition
	General	Place cursor anywhere within your document or the desired section when applying Page Setup values. Place the cursor within the desired paragraph or select several when applying paragraph settings.
1	Margins setting	Click to set all margins of your document.
2	Page size & orientation	Click to set paper dimensions and landscape or portrait orientation.
3	Margin value boxes	Enter values for each margin here; select with your mouse or tab between the margin value boxes. *Gutter* is the width from the magin to the inside (or *binding*) edge of a page.
4	Facing Pages	Check to apply different margins to even- and odd-numbered pages.
5	Apply To button	Click to apply the current margins to either the whole document or to a selected section (see Insert|Break Section Break).
6	Normal text	An example of text that runs from the left to the right margin.
7	Paragraph Indentation	Use (or drag the triangles at the left edge of the ruler) to set paragraph indentation. 7a—Controls/shows left margin setting; 7b—Controls/shows hanging indent setting (line two and higher). Drag with mouse; use **Shift** key as needed for proper operation. See shortcuts in item 8.
8	Indent From Left	Set Indentation From Left to 1.0". Shortcut: click the Indent icon on the toolbar or press **Ctrl+N**.
9	Indent From Left & Right	Set Indentation From Left and Indentation From Right to 1.0".
10	Indent First Line	Set Indentation First Line to 0.5".
11	Hanging Indent	Press **Ctrl+T** to apply a hanging indent. Press **Ctrl+G** to cancel.
12	Outdent	Set Indentation From Left to a negative value (such as -0.25") for an outdent; places text left of the left margin. Shortcut: click the Outdent icon on the toolbar.
13	Paragraph Alignment	Align text Left, Centered, Right, or Justified (same as alignment icons on the Toolbar). Shortcut keys are Ctrl+L, Ctrl+E, Ctrl+R, and Ctrl+J.
14	Paragraph Spacing	Use Spacing to set a fixed space before and after the selected paragraph(s); use *li* or *pt* (for lines or points).
15	Line Spacing	Use to set spacing between lines; to set 11 pt text on 12 pt spacing, use Line Spacing Exactly and enter 12 pt as a value.
16	Paragraph Pagination	Use as follows: Page Break Before forces paragraph to new page; Keep With Next keeps selected paragraph on the same page as following text; Keep Lines Together prevents undesired page breaks (typically prevents a break in a list resulting is what is called a *widow*).

32 Section 17—Setting Tabs

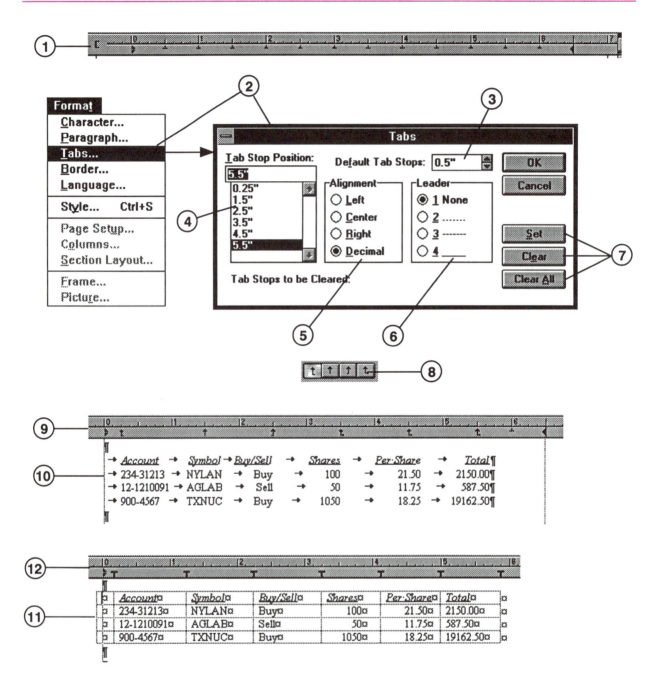

Section 17—Setting Tabs

Key	Description	Procedure or Definition
	General	Tab stops are displayed on the ruler. Four tab types are available and shown as icons on the ribbon (see item 8 below). From left to right, tab types include *Left* (or standard)—following text aligned flush left, *Center*—text centered beneath the tab stop, *Right*—text aligned flush right against the tab stop, and *Decimal*—decimals within numbers aligned beneath the decimal tab stop (for use with financial tables). Default tab stops are set at 0.5" increments. Inserting a tab stop eliminates default tab stops to the left. You can set tabs by positioning the cursor on the desired line in your document, picking the desired tab type on the ribbon, and picking the point on the ruler. You can also use the **Format|Tabs** dialog box to enter values, change default settings, and assign Leader attributes, i.e., dots, dashes, and underlines. Remove a tab by dragging it down and off the ruler or by picking it in the **Tabs** dialog box and clicking the Clear button.
1	Normal ruler	Default tab stops set on 0.5" spacing (shown as inverted "Ts").
2	Tabs dialog box	Access using the **Format|Tabs** menu or double click on a tab stop.
3	Default Tab Stops	Use this entry box to enter alternate default tab stop spacing.
4	Tab Stop Positions	With the cursor on the desired line in your document, type a tab stop value.
5	Tab Alignment	Pick a desired alignment for the highlighted (current) tab stop position.
6	Leaders	Pick a leader style. Leader 2 is often used with tables of contents.
7	Action buttons	Click Set to accept settings, Clear to remove a selected tab, and Clear All to clear all tab stops (this re-establishes default tab stop settings).
8	Tab icons (on ribbon)	Position the cursor on the line within your document, pick desired tab style icon, and then pick the tab stop position on the ruler.
9	Tab stop example	This ruler shows new tab stops as follows: Left at .25", Center at 1.5", Right at 2.5", and Decimal at 3.5", 4.5", and 5.5".
10	Tabbed text example	The body text of this table uses the tab stops shown in item 9; the line containing the headings uses Right tab stops for the last three headings.
11	Converted table example	This example shows the tabbed text in item 10 as converted to a table by selecting the tabbed text and using the **Table|Convert Text to Table** menu.
12	Table tabs	The inverted "Ts" are table tabs that control column boundaries. When tabbed text is converted to a table, these tab stops must be dragged to their proper positions.

Section 18—Formatting Text—Part 1 (Pages, Paragraphs, and Characters)

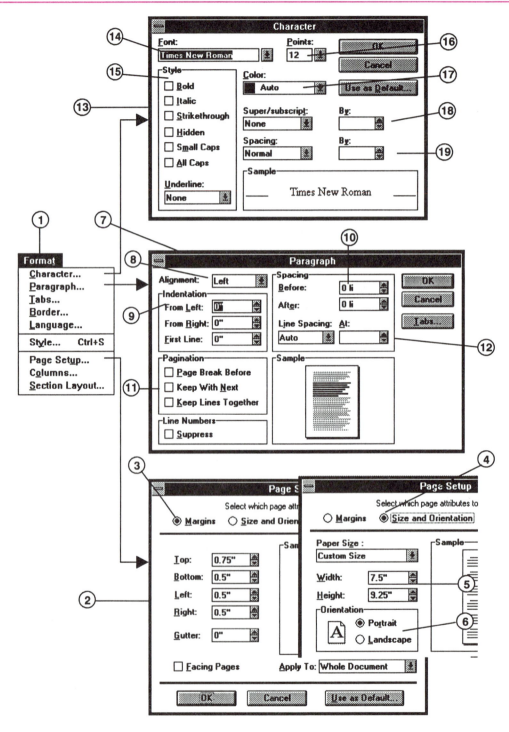

Section 18—Formatting Text—Part 1 (Pages, Paragraphs, and Characters)

Key	Description	Procedure or Definition
	General	The **Format** menu and the pictured dialog boxes are used to adjust page margins and sizes; paragraph alignment, indentation, and widow control; and character size, style, and spacing.
1	Format menu	Use this menu and the ribbon to set up the format of your documents.
2	Page Setup dialog box	Use to set margins and page size.
3	Margins	Enter distances from the top, bottom, left, and right edge of paper; use Gutter to set the inside (binding edge) margins if Facing Pages is checked. Gutters vary left and right with odd-and even-numbered pages.
4	Size and Orientation	Use to set the paper size and page orientation used.
5	Paper Size	Enter the page height and width; the default values are is 8.5" x 11".
6	Page Orientation	Pick Portrait (normal orientation) or Landscape to print sideways.
7	Paragraph dialog box	Use to establish indents and line spacing for selected paragraphs.
8	Paragraph Alignment	Set Left, Right, Centered, or Justified (or use toolbar icons)
9	Paragraph Indentation	Enter indentation value From Right, From Left, or for First Line.
10	Paragraph Spacing	Use to adjust spacing before and/or after the selected paragraph(s).
11	Paragraph Pagination	Use to keep lists together and to avoid undesired page breaks.
12	Paragraph Line Spacing	Alter the automatic spacing by lines or points; to set 11-point characters on 12-point spacing, type 12 pt in the Line Spacing At box.
13	Character dialog box	Use to set character font, style, size, subscript/superscript, and spacing.
14	Character Font	Enter font name for selected text; you can also set this with the ribbon.
15	Character Style	Check text style (bold, italic, strikethrough, etc.); use Underline to set a single or double underline and to prevent underlines beneath spaces.
16	Points (character size)	Enter a value or pick from list. This is an alternative to the point size selection on the ribbon. There are 72 points in an inch.
17	Character Color	Use to set the color of the selected passage.
18	Superscript/Subscript	Use to set text as superscript or subscript. The By value controls the distance above or below the baseline. The default is 3 points.
19	Character Spacing	Use to increase or decrease the horizontal space between characters. A sample is shown to help you determine the desired effect.

Section 19—Formatting Text—Part 2 (Sections)

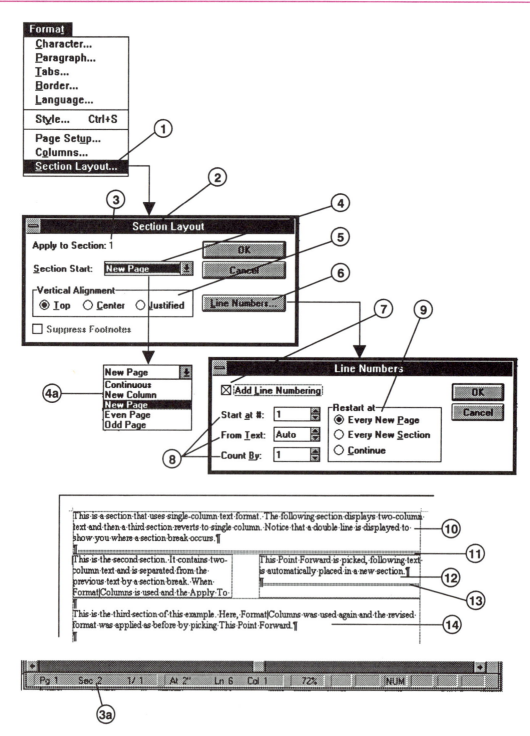

Section 19—Formatting Text—Part 2 (Sections)

Key	Description	Procedure or Definition
	General	Sections are used to separate different formats within a single document. For example, if you want to mix two or more columnar formats on the same page, each different format is placed in a new format. The example at the bottom of the illustration shows a small document that uses three sections.
1	Format|Section Layout menu	Use to start a new section. The **Format|Columns** menu also creates a new section when the columnar format is changed within a document.
2	Section Layout dialog box	Use to begin a new section, add line numbers to the printed document, and to align the text vertically within a section (see item 5).
3	Current section number	The selected section number is displayed here and on the status line (3a)
4	Section Start	Pick a starting point for the new section. See 4a for starting selections.
5	Vertical Alignment	Pick appropriate button to align text at the top, centered, or spread evenly from top to bottom. Use Print Preview to see the effect of Vertical Alignment.
6	Line Numbers button	Pick to display the Line Numbers dialog box.
7	Add Line Numbering	Check this box if you want to add line numbers to the printed document. Line numbers are not displayed on the screen.
8	Line Number format and placement	Pick a starting line number (Start at #), enter a From Text value to position the line numbers to the left of the text, and pick an increment (Count By). Count By 2 numbers lines 2, 4, 6, 8 and so on.
9	Restart at	Select a restarting point for line numbers. You can restart numbering on every new page, at the beginning of every section, or number continuously.
10	Section 1 example	Section 1 is one-column (margin to margin) text.
11	Section break example	The double lines indicates the boundary between sections 1 and 2.
12	Section 2 example	Notice that section 2 is a two-column passage.
13	Section break example	This section boundary occurs within a column.
14	Section 3 example	Section 3 resumes the one-column format.

Section 20—Numbered and Bulleted Lists

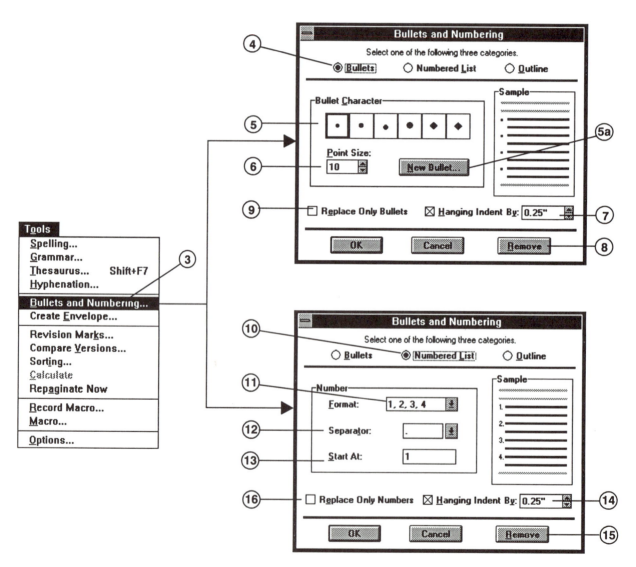

Section 20—Numbered and Bulleted Lists

Key	Description	Procedure or Definition
	General	Adding numbers or bullets to text is accomplished by selecting the desired text and then picking either the number or bullet icons on the toolbar. You can also use the **Tools|Bullets and Numbering** menu. Pick either Bullets or Numbered List and click OK. Numbers and bullets can be reformatted using the corresponding dialog boxes.
1	Numbered list	Example of a numbered list and the corresponding icon on the toolbar.
2	Bulleted list	Example of a bulleted list and the corresponding icon on the toolbar.
3	Tools|Bullets and Numbering	Pick this menu item to display the **Bullets and Numbering** dialog boxes. Picking the Bullets or Numbered List buttons displays variations of the dialog box. Pick Outline to adjust the style of an outline.
4	Bullets button	Pick to display selections that control bullet style and size.
5	Bullet Character	Pick either one of the six bullet styles shown or click the New Bullet button to select an alternate symbol.
6	Point Size	Use to increase or decrease the bullet size (in points).
7	Hanging Indent By	Use to change the space between the bullet and following text.
8	Remove button	Pick to remove bullets from the selected passage.
9	Replace Only Bullets	When the bullet style is changed, check this box to prevent adding bullets to lines not already having bullets.
10	Numbered List button	Pick to display selections that control the format of numbered lists.
11	Number Format	Pick alternate numbering formats including Arabic, Roman, and alphabetical.
12	Number Separator	Pick to change the period to other characters including single and double parentheses, colons, brackets, and double hyphens.
13	Number Start At	Pick a starting number; entering 10 omits 1 through 9.
14	Hanging Indent By	Use to change the space between the number and following text.
15	Remove button	Pick to remove numbers from the selected passage.
16	Replace Only Numbers	When the list is changed, check this box to prevent adding numbers to lines not already having numbers.

Section 21—Find and Replace

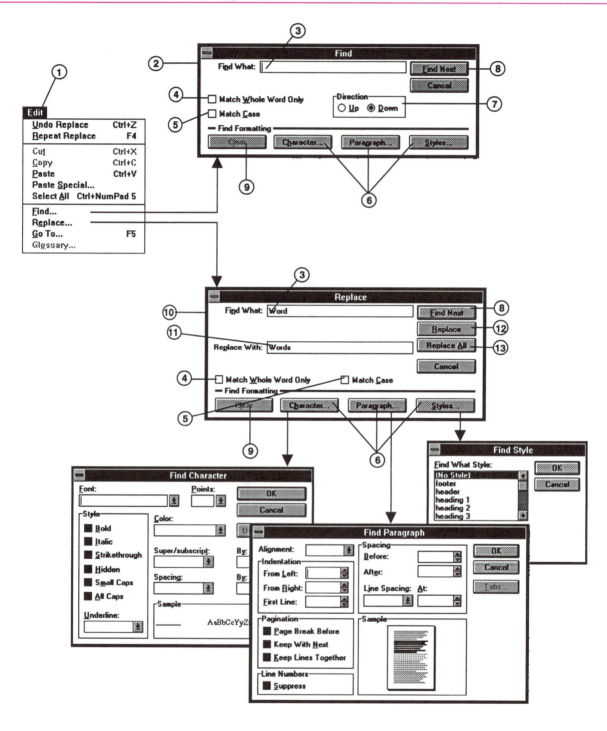

Section 21—Find and Replace

Key	Description	Procedure or Definition
	General	The Find and the Replace operations work similarly. They both begin at the current cursor position. Both let you find a word, passage, or special character within a document. Both let you restrict finds to whole words, special characters, formats, and/or styles. However, if you wish to replace a designated word or passage with another, use Replace.
1	Edit|Find and Edit|Replace menus	Pick the Find or Replace menu selection depending on your needs. Both find a designated entry; use Replace to replace one entry with another.
2	Find dialog box	Use to find a word, passage, or special character (or *entry*).
3	Find What box	Type the word, passage, or character you want to find or paste it from the clipboard.
4	Match Whole Word Only check box	Check to restrict your find to a whole word only. Otherwise, partial words, such as *there* in the word *therefore*, are found.
5	Match Case check box	Check to restrict your find to upper or lower case as entered.
6	Find Formatting buttons	Use to find special characters, paragraph formats, or styles using the corresponding dialog boxes shown at the bottom of the illustration.
7	Find Direction buttons	Pick to search forward or backward within the document.
8	Find Next button	Click to find the next occurrence of the find entry.
9	Clear button	Click to clear the current Find Formatting settings.
10	Replace dialog box	Use to find and replace a word, passage, or special character.
11	Replace With box	Type the word, passage, or character that replaces the Find What entry.
12	Replace button	Click to replace the Find What entry with the Replace With entry.
13	Replace All button	Click to replace all Find What entries with the Replace With entries.

Special Find Characters:

?—wild card (hel? finds hello, help, etc.)
^?—question mark (What^? finds What?)
^w—white space (spaces, etc.)
^t—tab
^p—paragraph mark
^n—end-of-line character
^d—page/section break
^m—duplicate find text
^c—clipboard contents
^s—nonbreaking space
^—word break hyphen
^~—nonbreaking hyphen
^0*nnn*—ANSI character

Finding ASCII Characters:

^*nnn*, where ^*nnn* are:
 ^1—graphic
 ^2—footnote
 ^3—footnote separator
 ^5—annotation mark
 ^9—tab
 ^10—linefeed
 ^12—page/section break
 ^13—paragraph mark
 ^14—column break
 ^19—{field code}

42 Section 22—Working with Tables—Part 1 (Table Creation)

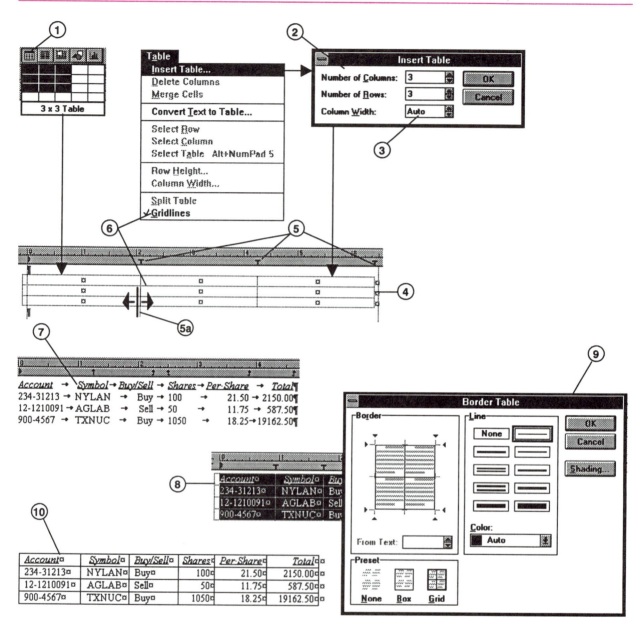

Section 22—Working with Tables—Part 1 (Table Creation)

Key	Description	Procedure or Definition
	General	Tables are created in three ways. First, you can create an empty table by clicking the table icon, highlighting the number of columns and rows, and releasing the mouse button. Similarly, use the **Table|Insert Table** menu, enter the number of columns and rows, the column width, and click OK. Finally, you can convert tabular text to a table by selecting it and picking the **Table|Convert Text to Table** selection.
1	Table icon	Pick, drag table row and column dimensions, and release mouse button. Also click this icon to create a table from selected tabular text.
2	Insert Table dialog box	Enter the Number of Columns, Number of Rows, and Column Width values and click OK to create a table at the cursor position.
3	Column Width	Leave "Auto" for equal spacing or enter a value such as 1.5".
4	Resulting table	A 3 X 3 table resulting from the settings shown in items 1 and 2.
5	Table tabs	Marks column boundaries. Drag right or left to adjust column widths. Alternately use the column cursor (5a) to adjust column widths. The column cursor is displayed when the mouse pointer is moved across a column intersection.
6	Gridlines	Turn on or off by picking **Table|Gridlines**.
7	Table|Convert Text to Table	Create a table as shown. Then select it and click the Table icon on the toolbar or pick **Table|Convert Text to Table**.
8	Table|Select Table	Once the table is converted from text, adjust the column widths by dragging the table tabs or column lines. To rule the table, select it by putting the cursor inside the table and picking **Select Table** or pressing **Alt+Num Pad 5**. Then use **Format|Border** as described in item 9.
9	Format|Border Table dialog box	To rule the table, select the Grid box, the desired line weight, and click OK.
10	Ruled table example	The result is a ruled table that resembles the example.

Section 23—Working with Tables—Part 2 (Editing Tables)

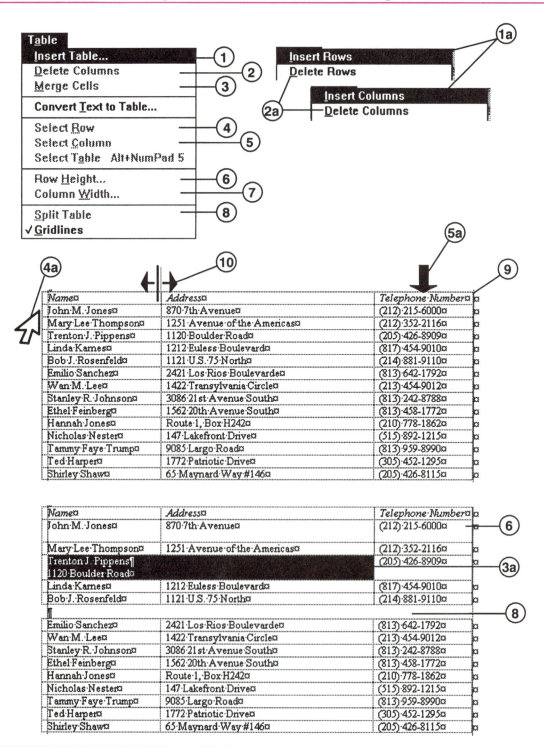

Section 23—Working with Tables—Part 2 (Editing Tables)

Key	Description	Procedure or Definition
	General	Table editing includes inserting and deleting rows and columns, splitting a table, and merging cells. These operations make use of the selections available in the **Table** menu. Use conventional editing procedures to edit text within tables. If you make a mistake while editing a table, press **Ctrl+Z** or use **Edit|Undo** to undo the last change.
1	Insert Cells/ Rows/ or Columns	Position the cursor and use **Table|Insert** to insert a cell, row, or column. The menu text changes with what is currently selected.
2	Delete Cells/ Rows/ or Columns	Select a cell, row, or column and use **Table|Delete** to delete a cell, row, or column. The menu text changes with what is currently selected.
3	Merge Cells	Select two or more adjacent cells and use **Table|Merge Cells** to combine the selected cells into a single cell. (See 3a.)
4	Select Row	Use to select a row for editing, or move the cursor to the left edge of a cell or row to alternately use the cell/row selection cursor shown in 4a.
5	Select Column	Use to select a column for editing or move the cursor above the column to alternately use the column selection cursor shown in 5a.
6	Row Height	Select a row and use the **Row Height** dialog box to change the height of a row.
7	Column Width	Select a column and use the **Column Width** dialog box to change the width of a column and the space between columns.
8	Split Table	Place the cursor in a cell; then pick **Table|Split Table** to divide the table above the cell in which the cursor is located.
9	Unedited table example	This illustrates the table before changes; immediately below is an edited table.
10	Column adjust cursor	This cursor, described in Section 22, is displayed when the mouse pointer approaches a column intersection. When displayed, drag the column boundary right or left to the desired position. You may alternately drag table tabs on the ruler to adjust column widths.

46 Section 24—Working with Columns

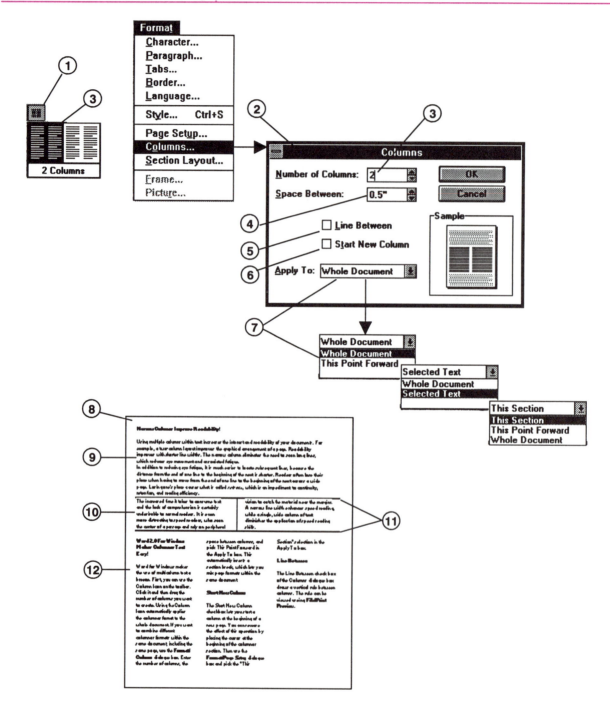

Section 24—Working with Columns

Key	Description	Procedure or Definition
	General	Two, three, or more columns of text are easily created using the Column icon (item 1) or the **Format|Columns** dialog box (item 2 and following). The column setting is applied to the whole document unless you specifically "tell" Word where to apply the column format. If a partial document is to be put in multicolumn format, select it before creating the columns.
1	Column icon	Select text or place cursor in a document section. Pick and drag the number of columns you want to use. The icon example shows 2 columns. The columnar format is automatically applied to the whole document.
2	Format|Columns dialog box	Use this dialog box to specify more details about your columns. This includes space between, vertical line, and what part of the document to apply the columnar format.
3	Number of Columns	Drag the icon or type a number to specify a number of columns.
4	Space Between	Enter the desired space between columns here; 0.3" works nicely.
5	Line Between check box	Click this box to insert an "X" if you want a vertical rule between columns.
6	Start New Column check box	Click this box to insert an "X" if you want to start the first column of the selected text on a new page.

7	Apply To box	Pick one of the following (choices vary with what is currently selected):
		    Whole Document—apply format to entire document.
		    This Point Forward—apply format to rest of document; this automatically inserts a new section.
		    Selected Text—apply format to highlighted (selected) text. This places section boundaries around the selected text.
		    This Section—apply format to current section.

8	Columnar text example	The example page shows three different formats on the same page.
9	Single-column text	The sample page begins with a single (default) column.
10	Two-column text	Select (highlight) the passage. Set up the Columns dialog box as follows: Number of Columns—2, Space Between—0.3", Line Between—X, Apply To—Selected Text. When set, pick OK.
11	Section boundaries	Section boundaries are automatically inserted around "Selected Text."
12	Three-column text	Put cursor at beginning of passage. Set the Columns dialog box as follows: Number of Columns—3, Space Between—0.3", and Apply To—This Point Forward.

Section 25—Working with Frames; Runarounds

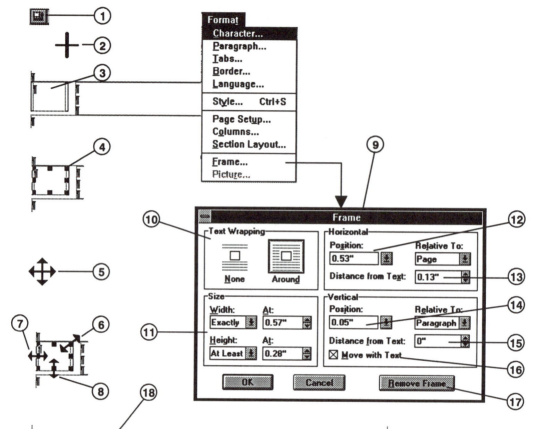

Section 25—Working with Frames; Runarounds

Key	Description	Procedure or Definition
	General	Use frames to insert pictures, boxed text (or *sidebars*), and newspaper style titles (or *mastheads*). You can insert frames inside frames. You can also add borders to frames using **Format|Border**. In general, you should enter a carriage return before inserting a frame.
1	Frame icon	Click to insert a frame; a frame cursor is displayed.
2	Frame cursor	Use to position and drag the size of a new frame.
3	Inserted frame	Notice how the text area around the frame is separated by space (called a *standoff*).
4	Frame "handles"	Click inside a frame to display handles used to resize the frame.
5	Frame cursor	Drag the frame to a new location using this cursor.
6	Width cursor	Drag to stretch the frame horizontally; press **Shift** to adjust border size.
7	Height cursor	Drag to stretch the frame vertically; press **Shift** to adjust border size.
8	Diagonal cursor	Drag to resize the frame proportionally; press **Shift** to adjust border size.
9	Format|Frame dialog box	Click a frame; then use this dialog box to adjust text wrapping, size, and vertical and horizontal spacing, or use to remove the active frame.
10	Text Wrapping	Click None to separate a frame from text; click Around to cause text to run around an inserted frame.
11	Size	Set the size of a frame here. Use Exactly to enter dimension values.
12	Horizontal Position	Set horizontal frame position relative to Margin, Page, or Column.
13	Distance from Text	Set horizontal space (or *standoff*) between frame and text.
14	Vertical Position	Set vertical frame position relative to Margin, Page, or Paragraph
15	Distance from Text	Set vertical space (or *standoff*) between frame and text.
16	Move with Text check box	An "X" keeps the frame in position relative to adjacent text; remove "X" to keep the frame in place relative to its position on the page.
17	Remove Frame button	Click to remove the selected frame from the document.
18	Frame example	Notice how the text runs around the frame. The distance between the frame and adjacent text is controlled by the values entered in the Distance from Text boxes within the **Frame** dialog box.

Section 26—Adding Borders and Lines

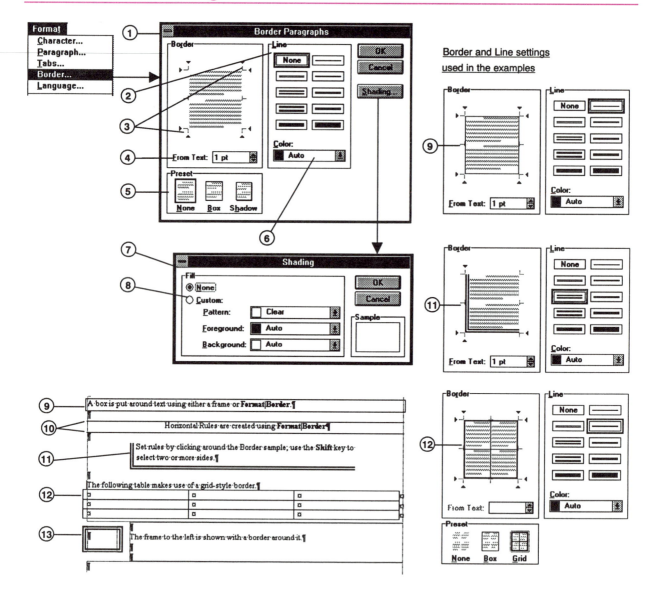

Section 26—Adding Borders and Lines

Key	Description	Procedure or Definition
	General	To draw a box-like border or one or more lines around one or more lines of text, a table, a frame, or even a header or footer, select the text and use the **Format|Border** menu and dialog box. Select the Border and Line styles and click OK. You can also select border colors and interior colors and shading using the **Border** dialog box.
1	Border Paragraphs dialog box	Use to set border and line styles, distance from text, and colors.
2	Lines selection	Pick the border line style; the active style is boxed.
3	Border selection	With None selected as the Line style, leave all sides marked for a full border. For one line, pick a side with the mouse pointer. For additional lines, press **Shift** and pick one or more additional sides. Once marked, pick the desired Line style and then click OK to see the results.
4	From Text	Enter a value to control the space between text and the border or line.
5	Preset (border type)	Pick a border style here; styles vary with what is selected.
6	Color	Pick a border color from a list of available colors.
7	Shading dialog box	Click the Shading button to display the **Shading** dialog box. Use this dialog box to pick shading for bordered text, tables, and frames.
8	None/Custom buttons	Pick a Pattern (screen percentage), a Foreground (screen) color, and a Background color to suit your needs. Check the sample for results.
9	Border around text	Example of a border around a single line of text.
10	Line above and beneath	Example of a line above and below a line of text.
11	Line beside and beneath	Example of a line beside and beneath a line of indented text.
12	Bordered table	Example of a border applied to a table and its cells; the Grid Preset is selected in this example to insert borders around each cell in the table.
13	Bordered frame	Example of a border around a frame. Just pick the frame to display the handles; then add a border of your choosing.

52 Section 27—Headers and Footers

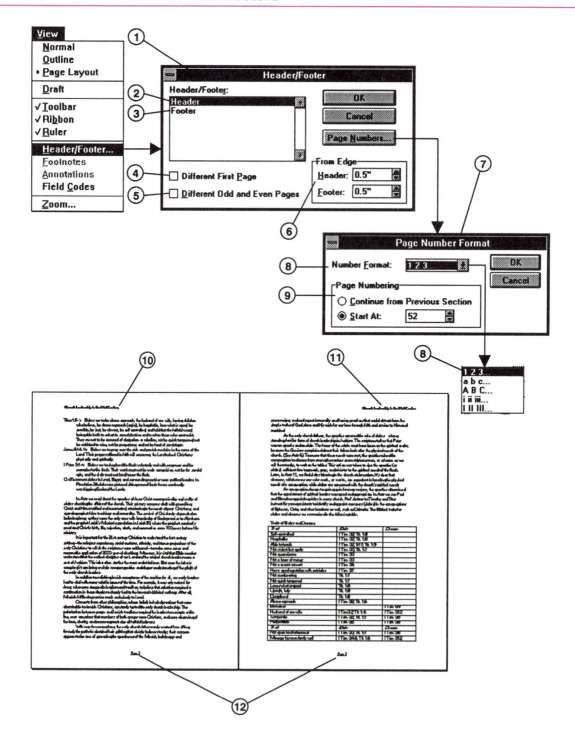

Section 27—Headers and Footers

Key	Description	Procedure or Definition
	General	Use the **View|Header/Footer** menu and dialog box to insert a header, footer, or both. Headers and footers can be varied by odd and even page. Also, the first page of a document can be different from following pages. For example, you can suppress the page number or a header on the first page of a document, such as a title page or a chapter opening.
1	Header/Footer dialog box	Use the controls within this dialog box to adjust the way your headers and footers are displayed on your document including the distance from the page boundaries and embedded page numbers.
2	Header	Pick this selection to choose your header settings.
3	Footer	Pick this selection to choose your footer settings.
4	Different First Page	Check if the first page of your document varies from the other pages.
5	Different Odd and Even Pages	Check if you want odd and even numbered page headers/footers to differ. The example makes use of this check box; the headers alternate flush left and flush right to display at the outside edge of each page.
6	Distance From Edge	Set the distance from the outside edges of the page.
7	Page Number Format dialog box	Use the controls in this dialog box to pick the page number style, sequence, and a beginning page number.
8	Number Format	Pick the desired page number format from the displayed pick list.
9	Page Numbering	Select continuous page numbers or start a new sequence in the current section.
10	Even # page header	Example of a left-hand (even numbered) page header. Check the Different Odd and Even Pages box to achieve this effect.
11	Odd # page header	Example of a right-hand (odd numbered) page header. Note that this header is formatted flush right by picking the Flush Right icon or pressing **Ctrl+R**.
12	Footers that include page # fields	Example of footers that include page numbers. The page number was added using **Insert|Field** and picking Page from the list.

54 Section 28—Footnotes and Annotations

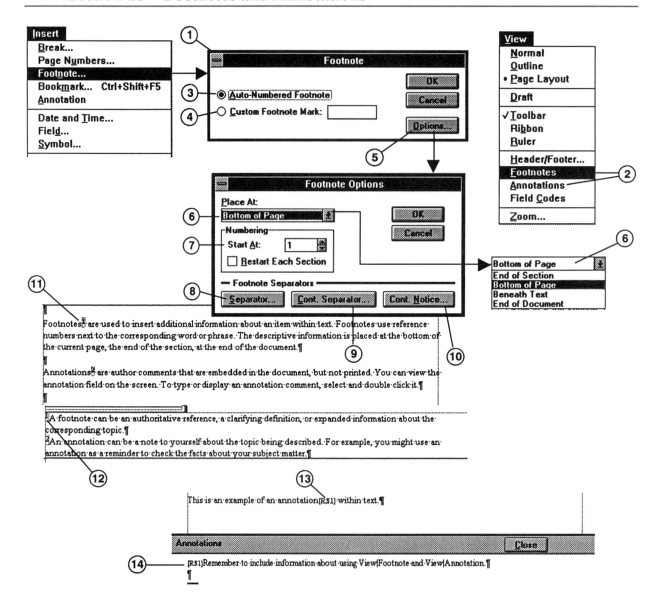

Section 28—Footnotes and Annotations

Key	Description	Procedure or Definition
	General	Footnotes are used to insert expanded information about an item found in text. Footnotes use reference numbers next to the corresponding word or phrase. The descriptive information is placed at the bottom of the current page, the end of the section, or at the end of the document. Annotations are author comments that are embedded in the document, but not printed. You can view annotation fields on the screen. To type or display an annotation comment, select and double click it. You can also use **View|Annotations** or **View|Footnotes** to access contents.
1	Insert|Footnote dialog box	Pick automatic numbering, a custom mark, or access special options.
2	View|Footnotes and View|Annotations	Pick **View|Footnotes** to display footnote text; pick **View|Annotations** to display annotation text.
3	Auto Numbered Footnote	Pick this button (the default selection) to increment footnote numbers by 1 automatically.
4	Custom Footnote Mark	Enter a custom footnote mark of your own, such as an asterisk, here.
5	Footnote Options button	Pick to display the **Footnote Options** dialog box, which offers various placement, numbering, and separator options.
6	Place At	Pick Bottom of Page, End of Section, End of Document, or Beneath text.
7	Numbering Start At	Select a starting number for the first footnote. The default is 1. Check the Restart Each Section box to restart the number sequence at the beginning of each section in the document.
8	Separator button	Click to alter the separator line between document text and footnote.
9	Cont. Separator button	Click to draw a continuation separator below the footnote text.
10	Cont. Notice button	Click to type a continuation notice following the footnote text. Use **File|Page Preview** to view the footnote layout.
11	Footnote mark	An example of a footnote mark within the text of a document.
12	Footnote text	An example of footnote text.
13	Annotation mark	An example of an annotation mark; the initials are controlled using **Tools|Options|User Info**.
14	Annotation text	An example of annotation text, which is a note to the document author.

56 Section 29—Page Numbers and Dates

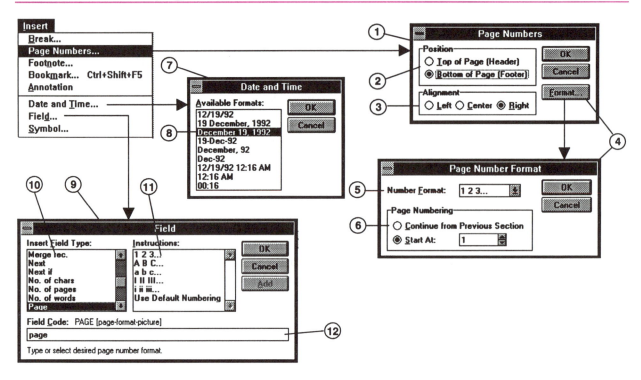

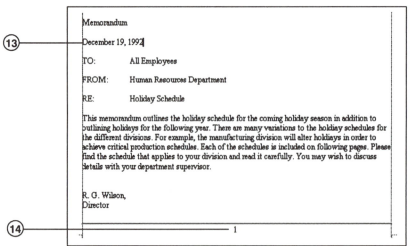

Section 29—Page Numbers and Dates

Key	Description	Procedure or Definition
	General	Place page numbers within either a footer or a header of your document using the **Insert|Page Numbers** menu and dialog box. You can also add page numbers using the **Insert|Field** menu and pick Page from the list of field types. Use **Insert|Date and Time** to display the current system date and/or time in your text. Here again, you can use the **Insert|Field** menu and pick Date or Time from the list of field types.
1	Insert|Page Numbers	Use this menu and dialog box to position and format your page numbers.
2	Page No. Position	Pick the page number location (Header or Footer) here.
3	Page No. Alignment	Pick Left, Center, or Right to place your page number horizontally.
4	Page No. Format	Pick a page number format and set the starting number here.
5	Number Format	Pick the suitable format (Arabic, alphabetical, or Roman) here.
6	Page Numbering	Pick to continue page numbers from a previous section or restart the sequence and enter the starting number in the text box.
7	Insert|Date and Time	Pick this menu item to display the **Date and Time** dialog box.
8	Available Formats list	Pick either the current date or time format of your choice from this list. The resulting date or time is based on your computer's system clock.
9	Insert|Field	Pick to display the **Field** dialog box.
10	Insert Field Type list	Pick a field type; typing the first letter of a listed item, such as **P**, jumps directly to the Page entry within the list.
11	Instructions list	Pick an appropriate format from the Instructions list.
12	Field Code box	View and/or edit the format of the selected field type here.
13	Date example	This is the result of an **Insert|Date and Time** operation using the U.S. date format which is the third item in the Available Formats list.
14	Page number example	This page number is a centered footer on the example page. Note that you can expand the footer by typing **Page {PAGE} of 5**, where {PAGE} is the page field code within your footer.

Section 30—Bookmarks (Finding Your Place)

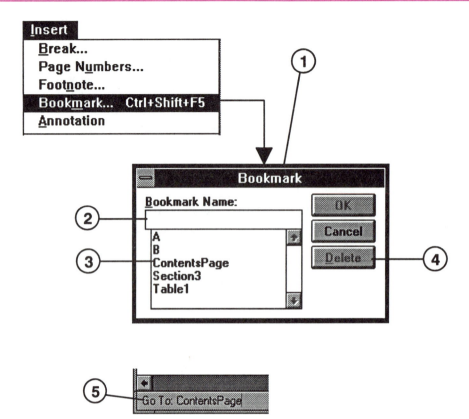

Section 30—Bookmarks (Finding Your Place) 59

Key	Description	Procedure or Definition
	General	Use the **Insert|Bookmark** menu selection to insert bookmarks (or *place holders*) within a document at the cursor location. Bookmark names can be one or more characters, must start with an alphabetical letter, and never include spaces. Bookmarks provide an excellent way to jump directly to a location within a large document. Just press **F5**, type a bookmark name (or a page number), and jump directly to a bookmark (or page). A bookmark name can also be applied to an entire passage. This allows you to insert selected passages from one document to another. Do this by positioning your cursor at the insertion point. Then use **Insert|File**, pick the filename, type the bookmark name in the Range box, and click OK.
1	Insert|Bookmark	Pick this menu item to display the **Bookmark** dialog box or use **Ctrl+Shift+F5**, which is the equivalent shortcut key sequence.
2	Bookmark Name box	Type an appropriate bookmark name here.
3	Bookmark Name list	View the list of existing bookmark names, if any, here. Names are alphabetized to make finding them easy.
4	Bookmark Delete button	Delete a bookmark name by picking (highlighting) the desired name and then clicking the Delete button.
5	Go To entry area	Press **F5** (the *Go To* key), type a bookmark name or a page number, and press **Enter** to jump to the bookmark or page. The Go To entry area is located at the bottom left corner on the status line.

60 Section 31—Inserting Special Characters and Symbols

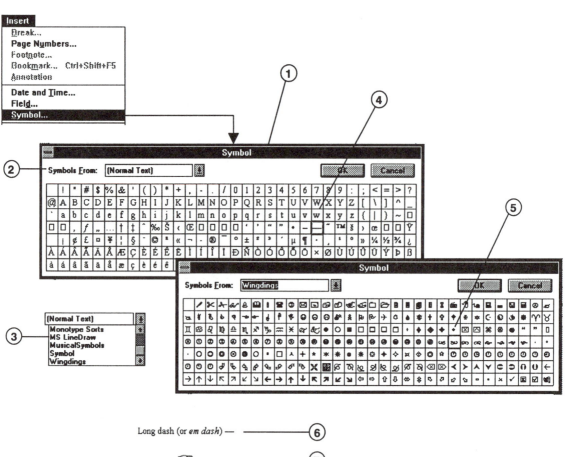

6. Long dash (or *em dash*) —
7.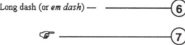
8. Various border symbols (from Wingdings)

   ෮෮෮෮෮෮෮෮෮
9.
   Character Map

Section 31—Inserting Special Characters and Symbols

Key	Description	Procedure or Definition
	General	Use the **Insert|Symbol** menu selection to display the **Symbol** dialog box (**Alt+I+S** is the shortcut key sequence). Use the **Symbol** dialog box to display different sets of special characters and symbols. Pick available symbol sets using the Symbols From pick list. Enlarge the display of a symbol by picking and holding the left mouse button. Once you pick a desired character or symbol, click OK (or double click it with your mouse). The selection is inserted at the current cursor position. You can copy and paste inserted symbols in the usual manner.
1	Symbols dialog box	Pick a symbol set and the symbol within the set that you want to use.
2	Symbols From box	Pick to display a list of names that correspond to available symbol sets.
3	Symbol From pick list	Pick a symbol set name you want to view and/or use.
4	Normal text symbols	This is an example of the Normal (default) symbol set.
5	Wingdings symbols	This is an example of the Wingdings symbol set, which contains a number of special symbols. Enlarge the point size as necessary (use **Ctrl+F2** to nudge one point at a time) until the size is satisfactory. (Use **Shift+Ctrl+F2** to reduce the size by one point.)
6	Long dash symbol	A commonly used symbol that is inserted within normal text.
7	Pointing hand symbol	A Wingdings symbol that is commonly used to highlight an item within text.
8	Border symbols	A combination of several Wingdings symbols used to create a decorative border or break within a document. You might use this technique in an announcement or completion certificate.
9	Windows Character Map accessory	More special characters and symbols are accessed using the Windows Character Map accessory. Copy a symbol to the clipboard and then paste it into your Word document.

Section 32—Dot Leaders

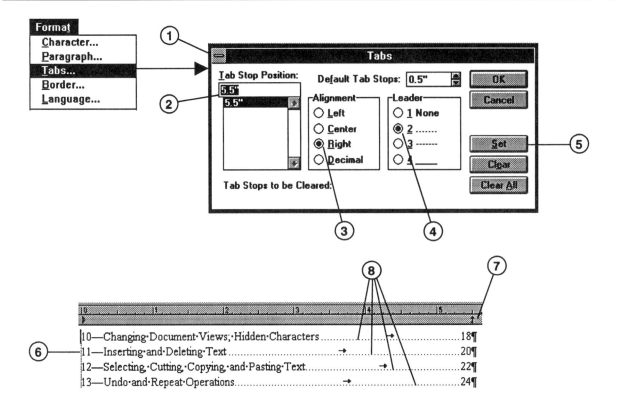

Section 32—Dot Leaders

Key	Description	Procedure or Definition
	General	Section 17 of this book describes the process of setting tabs and the use of the **Tabs** dialog box. This section reviews the use of *dot leaders*, which is a row of dots used to make it easy to line up adjoining entries, as in a table of contents. Setting a tab with a dot, dash, or underline style leader inserts the dots, dashes, or an underline character when you approach the tab setting by pressing the Tab key. The supporting illustrations shows you how to set up a flush right tab with the dot style leader. This is ideal for tables of contents as it keeps your page numbers properly aligned.
1	Tabs dialog box	Pick **Insert|Tabs** to display the **Tabs** dialog box.
2	Tab Stop Position	Type the tab position here. You can also pick the appropriate tab style using the Tab icons on the ribbon. When set, the tab stop settings are displayed in the Tab Stop Position list.
3	Alignment	Pick a tab alignment (Left, Center, Right, Decimal) setting. Alignment button 3 is picked in the example for Right.
4	Leader	Pick a Leader style; pick Leader button 2 for dots.
5	Set button	Pick the Set button once all settings (position, alignment, and leader) are ready.
6	Dot leader example	This example illustrates lines that are typical of a table of contents. The example corresponds to the settings in the **Tabs** dialog box shown in the illustration.
7	Flush right tab on ruler	The flush right tab corresponds to the setting in the **Tabs** dialog box.
8	Dot leaders	The resulting dot leaders are displayed and printed. Notice how the leader guides your eyes from the text to the corresponding page number.

Section 33—Indexes and Tables of Contents

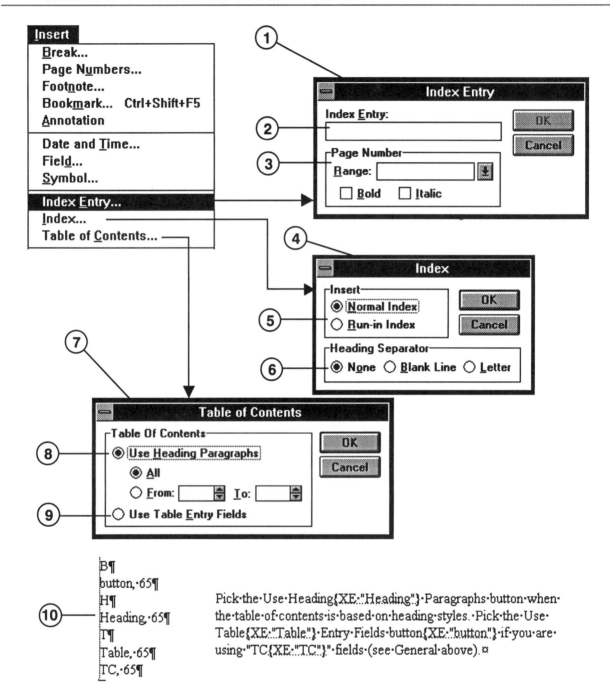

Section 33—Indexes and Tables of Contents

Key	Description	Procedure or Definition

	General	Create an index by first selecting each word (up to 64 characters), picking **Insert|Index Entry**, and clicking OK. You can also type a synonym of your own in the Index Entry box. Once the index entries are selected, position the cursor and pick **Insert|Index**, select a heading separator, and click OK to insert an alphabetized index at the cursor.
		
		Create a table of contents from established heading styles or by inserting table of contents fields. The fields, which should be inserted after the corresponding item in text, are entered by using **Insert|Field**, picking TC, and then clicking OK. The field formats are:
		
		    First level field: {tc "Text"}
		    Second level field {tc "Text"\L2}
		    Third level field {tc "Text"\L3}
		
		where Text is any table of contents entry.

1	Index Entry dialog box	Use the **Insert|Index Entry** dialog box to identify each index entry. Select entries within text or type your own synonym.
2	Index Entry text box	Displays selected text or lets you type your own index entry.
3	Page Number	Insert a bookmark name that corresponds to the desired range of pages. Check Bold or Italic to print the index page numbers accordingly.
4	Index dialog box	Use the **Insert|Index** dialog box to create your final alphabetical index. It is inserted at the current cursor location.
5	Insert buttons	Pick Normal Index to include all index entries in your compilation.
6	Heading Separator buttons	Pick the separation you want between each alphabetical entry. Pick None for no separator, Blank Line for a single line separation, or Letter for the first letter of the following series.
7	Table of Contents dialog box	Use **Insert|Table of Contents** to create a table of contents, which is inserted at the current cursor location.
8	Use Heading Paragraphs button	Pick this button when the table of contents is based on heading styles, i.e., Heading 1, 2, 3, etc.
9	Use Table Entry Fields button	Pick this button if you are using "TC" fields (see General above).
10	Index example	Notice how the example uses typed index entries {XE "*text*"} and the Letter Heading Separator in the corresponding passage.

Section 34—Spelling Checks

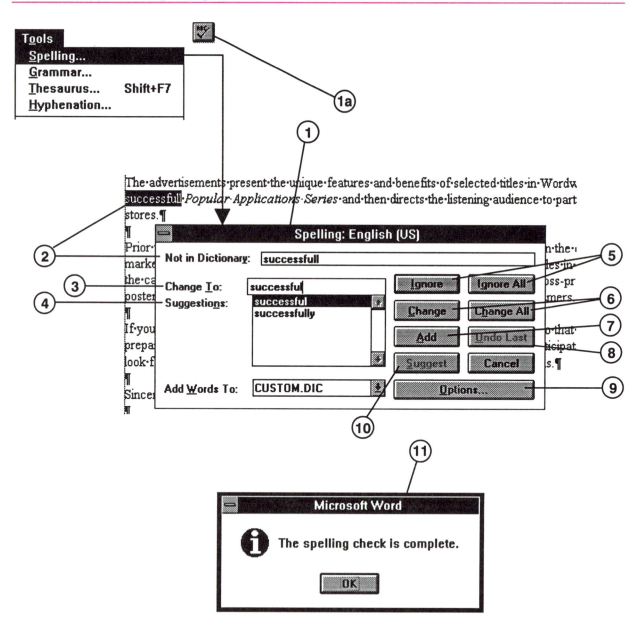

Section 34—Spelling Checks

Key	Description	Procedure or Definition
	General	Use Word's spelling checker to find misspelled words and typographical errors. Position the cursor or select one or more words. Then pick the Spell Check icon on the toolbar (see the icon at the top of the illustration) or pick **Tools|Spelling**. Pick the Change or Ignore buttons as necessary to process the word. If it is legitimate, pick Add to include the challenged word in your personal dictionary, which has the filename CUSTOM.DIC. You may also add and use other custom dictionaries.
1	Spelling dialog box	Access using **Tools|Spelling** or the Spelling icon (1a). Then use the buttons and text box to control the progress of your spelling check.
2	Challenged word	The challenged word is displayed in the dialog box and highlighted in text.
3	Change To suggestion	The first suggestion; you can type an alternative here.
4	Suggestions	Other suggestions are listed here.
5	Ignore and Ignore All buttons	Pick Ignore to bypass the current challenged word; pick Ignore All to bypass all instances of the challenged word, such as a proper name.
6	Change and Change All buttons	Pick Change to change the current challenge; pick Change All to change the challenged word throughout the text.
7	Add button	Pick Add to add the challenged word to your custom dictionary.
8	Undo Last button	Pick to undo the most recent word change.
9	Options button	Pick to display additional choices including the ability to ignore all uppercase words, words with numbers, and to either display or suppress suggestions.
10	Suggest button	When suggestions are suppressed using the Options dialog box, this button is used to display possible word choices.
11	Completion dialog box	This dialog box is displayed when the entire document is checked. If a partial spelling check is conducted, the dialog box is expanded to suggest that you check from the beginning of the document.

68 Section 35—Grammar Checks

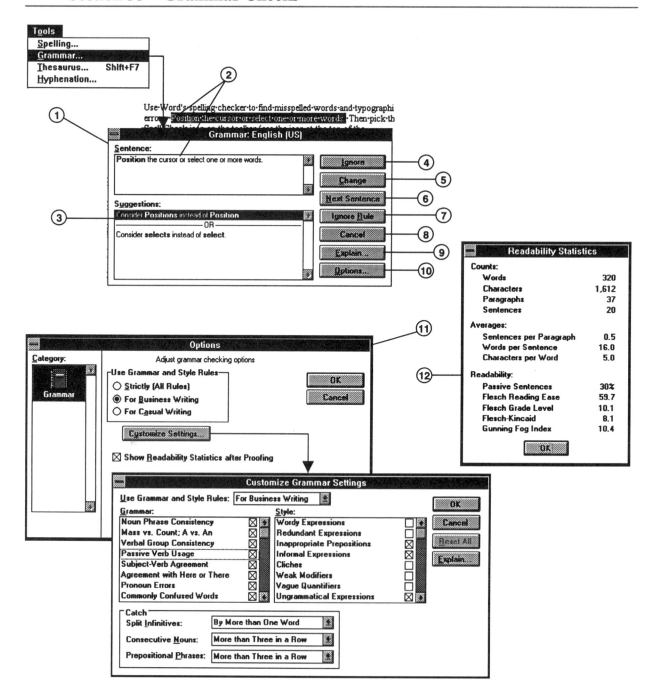

Section 35—Grammar Checks

Key	Description	Procedure or Definition
	General	The **Tools|Grammar** menu selection is used to examine grammar- and style-related characteristics, such as subject-verb agreement, passive verb agreement, double negatives, the use of jargon or clichés, and much more. It also performs a spelling check. Use the **Grammar** selection of the **Tools|Options** menu selection to set up the way your grammar check works. Pick the Customize Settings button to select which items to include or exclude in the grammar check. The check is performed from the cursor position to the end of the document, or you can restrict your check to a selected passage of text. Grammar statistics (item 11) are displayed when the grammar check is completed.
1	Grammar dialog box	Use this box to control the progress of a grammar and style check.
2	Sentence	The sentence being checked is displayed in the dialog box and highlighted in text.
3	Suggestions	Word suggests possible improvements; while several may be valid suggestions, some may not apply.
4	Ignore button	Pick to ignore the current suggestion.
5	Change button	Pick to change a misspelled word.
6	Next Sentence button	Pick to move to the next sentence in the passage being checked.
7	Ignore Rule button	Pick to disable the rule currently being applied.
8	Cancel button	Pick to cancel the grammar check.
9	Explain button	Pick to display a brief explanation about the suggestion.
10	Options button	Pick to change the grammar check parameters; this displays the same **Grammar Options** dialog box that is displayed using the **Tools|Options** menu.
11	Options dialog box	Review and modify the grammar check parameters here. Use the Customize Settings button to display the **Customize Grammar Settings** dialog box and set the rules to include in the check.
12	Readability Statistics	Review the statistics to see readability information about the checked passage. In addition to a character and word count, three recognized readability indexes are presented including the Flesch, Flesch-Kincade, and Gunning Fog index.

Section 36—Using the Thesaurus

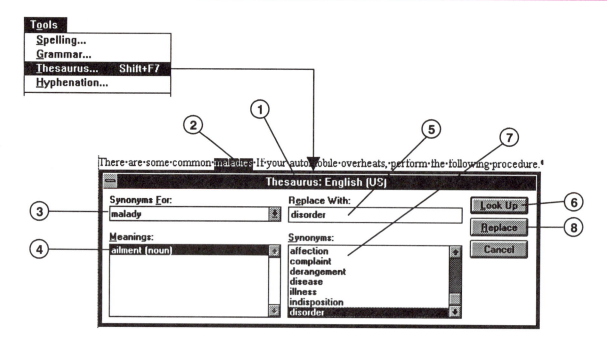

Section 36—Using the Thesaurus

Key	Description	Procedure or Definition
	General	Use **Tools|Thesaurus** to look up the meaning of a selected word and, if appropriate, to replace it with a *synonym*. (A synonym is a word having the same or a similar meaning to a selected word.) You can display definitions of the selected word and pick the Look Up button to display a list of synonyms.
1	Thesaurus dialog box	Use to display the meaning and synonyms for a selected word.
2	Selected word in text	The selected word is shown in context. A word is selected by positioning the cursor in front of it or by selecting the entire word.
3	Synonyms For box	The selected word is displayed here.
4	Meanings list	One or more probable meanings for the selected word are displayed here.
5	Replace With box	The currently selected synonym. The displayed synonym is used to replace the selected word when the Replace button is picked.
6	Look Up button	Pick this button to display (or "look up") a list of synonyms.
7	Synonyms pick list	Pick the synonym you want to use from this list. The highlighted synonym is displayed in the Replace With box.
8	Replace button	Pick this button to change the selected word to the synonym displayed in the Replace With box.

Section 37—Using Hyphenation

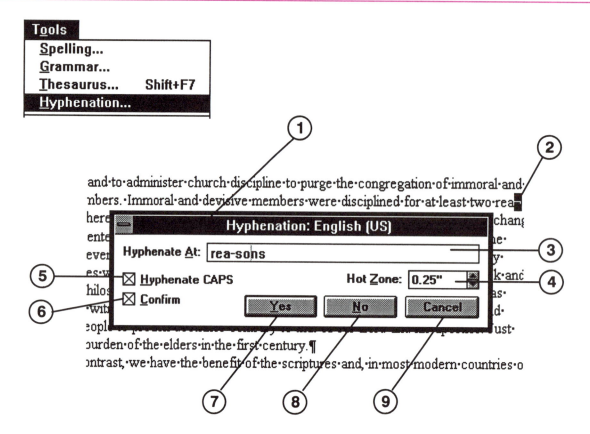

Section 37—Using Hyphenation

Key	Description	Procedure or Definition
	General	Position the cursor at the beginning of the text that you want to hyphenate or select (highlight) a passage. Then use the **Tools|Hyphenation** menu to display the **Hyphenation** dialog box. Here, you can set the width of the end-of-line "hot zone" as well as other hyphenation parameters. Click the OK button (which changes to a Yes button) to begin the hyphenation process. Word checks words to see where end-of-line hyphens can be inserted within the hot zone.
1	Hyphenation dialog box	Use this dialog box to control the settings and progress of the hyphenation process.
2	Selected word in text	The candidate word is highlighted in text so you can see it.
3	Hyphenate At box	Check and select alternate hyphenation points here. The hyphenation point is moved using the mouse.
4	Hot Zone	Set the width at the end of lines that you want scanned for possible hyphenation.
5	Hyphenate CAPS check box	Click this box to display an "X" to hyphenate capitalized words. Otherwise, capitalized words are omitted from the hyphenation process.
6	Confirm check box	Each hyphenation decision is displayed when this box is checked. Hyphenation proceeds automatically when the Confirm check box is empty.
7	Yes button	Pick to insert the hyphenation shown in the Hyphenate At box.
8	No button	Pick to retain the selected word without hyphenation.
9	Cancel button	Pick to discontinue the hyphenation process.

Section 38—Opening Multiple Documents with the Window Menu

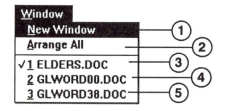

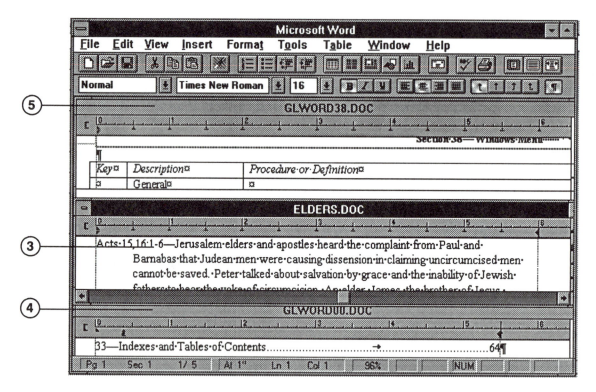

Section 38—Opening Multiple Documents with the Window Menu 75

Key	Description	Procedure or Definition
	General	The **Window** menu is used to display different documents at the same time in their own windows. You can also display different portions of the same document in more than one window. This lets you examine and move or copy passages or pictures from one document to another or from one location to another within the same document. You can achieve similar results by opening multiple documents and then using the Restore button (double triangle in the upper right-hand corner) to reduce a full-screen document to a window. Windows can be enlarged, shrunk, or moved to suit your needs. To resize, drag the borders or corners using the double-headed arrow. To move, pick the title bar and drag to the desired position.
1	Window|New Window	Pick to open the currently active document into a second window.
2	Window|Arrange All	Pick to arrange all open documents into evenly sized windows.
3	Window|1	Pick to access the corresponding document; you can also use **Alt+F6** to move between document windows or simply pick the document window with your mouse pointer. Notice the check mark. It designates the active document. Also notice that the menu bar of the active document is highlighted.
4	Window|2	Pick to access the corresponding document or click the document window with your mouse.
5	Window|3	Pick to access the corresponding document or click the document window with your mouse. Notice that this is the last open document in the list. Additional documents can be opened at the same time and are assigned the next available number.

Section 39—Automating Your Work with Macros

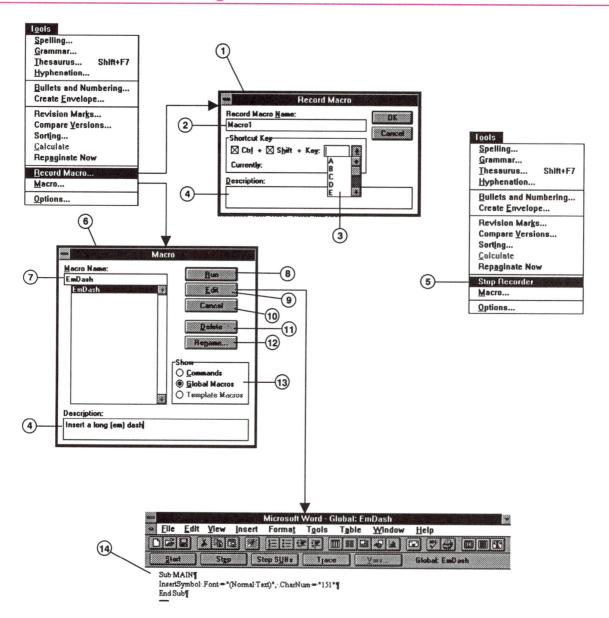

Section 39—Automating Your Work with Macros

Key	Description	Procedure or Definition
	General	A *macro* is a recording of keystrokes and/or mouse clicks that can be saved and played. Macros are ideal for frequently used operations, as they save you time. The **Tools|Record Macro** and **Tools|Macro** menu selections are used to record, play, and edit macros. The general process includes using **Record Macro** to name and record the involved keystrokes. **Tools|Stop Recorder** is used to end macro recording. Macros are run using established shortcut keys or by clicking the Run button in the **Tools|Macro** dialog box. Macros can be edited and saved like a document using the Edit button in the **Tools|Macro** dialog box.
1	Record Macro dialog box	Pick to name a new macro and to begin recording all following keystrokes and mouse clicks. This menu item changes to Stop Recorder during macro recording activity.
2	Record Macro Name box	Type a macro name here. The default name "Macro1" is displayed. Just type over it with a meaningful name of your own.
3	Shortcut Key	Pick a letter from the list. Once recorded, start the macro using **Ctrl+Shift+x**, where *x* is an available letter.
4	Description box	If you wish, you can type a description of your macro here.
5	Tools|Stop Recorder	Pick this menu item to end the recording process.
6	Macro dialog box	Pick to list macro names and to run, edit, rename, or delete a macro.
7	Macro Name box	Pick a macro from the list of names or type a name in this box.
8	Run button	Pick to run the selected macro.
9	Edit button	Pick to edit the contents of the selected macro. See item 14.
10	Cancel button	Pick to cancel the operation.
11	Delete button	Pick to delete the selected macro.
12	Rename button	Pick to rename the selected macro.
13	Show buttons	Pick to show macro options; Commands displays built-in Word macros, Global Macros displays macros saved in the NORMAL.DOT style sheet, and Template Macros displays macros in the current template (not in NORMAL.DOT).
14	Macro text example	This is a recorded macro that is displayed with the Macro Edit button. The macro displays a long dash symbol using the **Insert|Symbol** menu. You can edit and save a macro just like a regular document. Notice the special buttons. These are used to test and debug the displayed macro.

Section 40—Print Preview

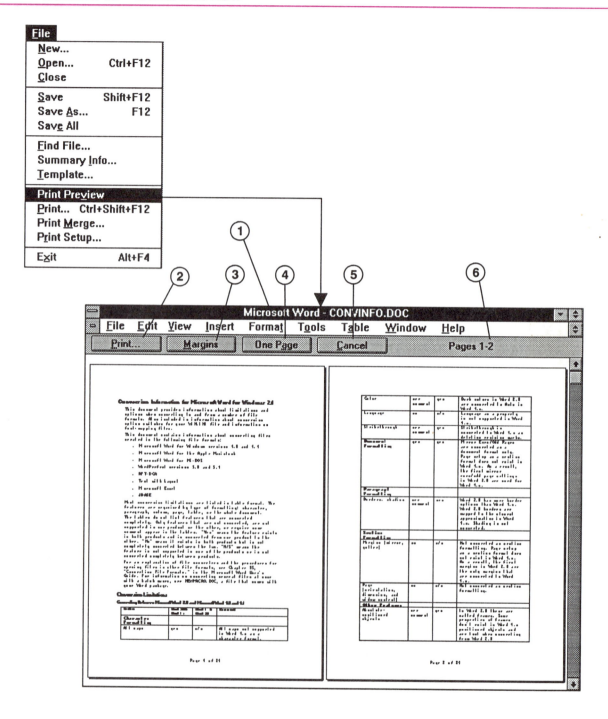

Section 40—Print Preview

Key	Description	Procedure or Definition
	General	Before printing a document, you can use the **File|Print Preview** selection to display the document as it should look when printed. You can also use **Print Preview** to see footnotes, borders, and lines that do not appear on the editing screen. You can also display two facing pages to check for a balanced page layout. To preview following or previous pages in a multipage document, press the **PgDn** or **PgUp** keys. Use **Ctrl+Home** to move to the first page and **Ctrl+End** to move the last page. When exiting Print Preview, Word returns you to the normal document editing screen at the currently previewed page.
1	Print Preview display	Pick **File|Print Preview** to display an on-screen simulation of what the current document will look like when printed.
2	Print button	Pick the Print button to print the displayed document.
3	Margins button	Pick the Margins button to display margin guidelines on the previewed page. You can drag displayed handles to modify the margin settings, which changes the margin values in the **Format|Page Setup** dialog box. You can move the guidelines to another page by clicking the page with your mouse.
4	One (or Two) Page(s) button	Pick the One Page button to preview a single page. When one page is displayed, this button is renamed "Two Pages."
5	Cancel (or Close) button	Pick the Cancel button to return to the normal document editing screen. This button is renamed "Close" when a modification is made to the previewed page (see item 3 above).
6	Page number(s)	The current page numbers are displayed here.

Section 41—Printing Operations—Part 1

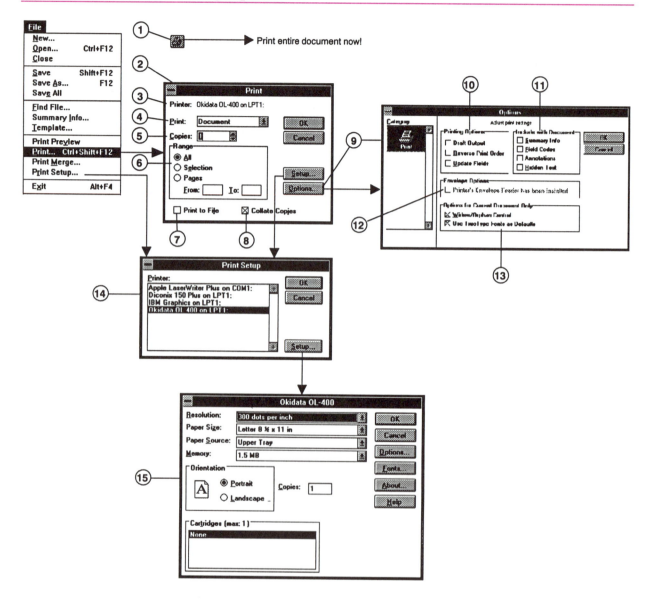

Section 41—Printing Operations—Part 1

Key	Description	Procedure or Definition
	General	Printing is achieved using **File|Print** and then picking the selections available in the **Print** dialog box. You can change the active printer using **File|Print Setup** or by clicking the Setup button in the **Print** dialog box. Once the setup is complete, click OK to begin printing. You can pick the Print icon (item 1) to print all pages of the current document using the established print defaults. This method omits the use of the **Print** dialog box. See Section 42 to see how to use the **File|Find** menu to print multiple documents.
1	Print icon	Click to print the active document using default printer settings.
2	Print dialog box	Use this dialog box to control the way your document prints.
3	Printer	The name of the currently installed Windows printer is displayed here.
4	Print	Pick the down arrow and select Document (the default), Summary Info, Annotations, Styles, Glossary, or Key Assignments.
5	Copies	Enter a number that corresponds to the number of copies to be printed.
6	Range options	Pick All, Current Page, or select a range of pages here; Current Page changes to "Selection" when a passage of text or an object is selected.
7	Print to File check box	Pick this box to "print" your document to a file instead of the printer.
8	Collate Copies check box	Pick this box to print each copy of your document in page number order.
9	Options dialog box	Pick this button to access the **Options** dialog box. This box is also accessed by picking Print from the **Tools|Options** menu.
10	Printing options check boxes	Check the boxes as required for Draft, Reverse Order printing, and to Update Fields within the document.
11	Include options check boxes	Check the boxes to include printing of Summary Info, Field Codes, Annotations, and/or Hidden Text.
12	Envelope options check box	Check this box if your printer has an envelope feeder. Otherwise, envelopes must be fed manually.
13	Document options check boxes	Check for Widow/Orphan control (to omit isolated elements) and to select the use of True Type fonts as the default.
14	Print Setup dialog box	Pick the Setup button to select an installed Windows printer. This dialog box is accessed directly using the **File|Print Setup** menu.
15	Setup dialog box	Use this dialog box to control settings that are specific to the active Windows printer.

Section 42—Printing Operations—Part 2

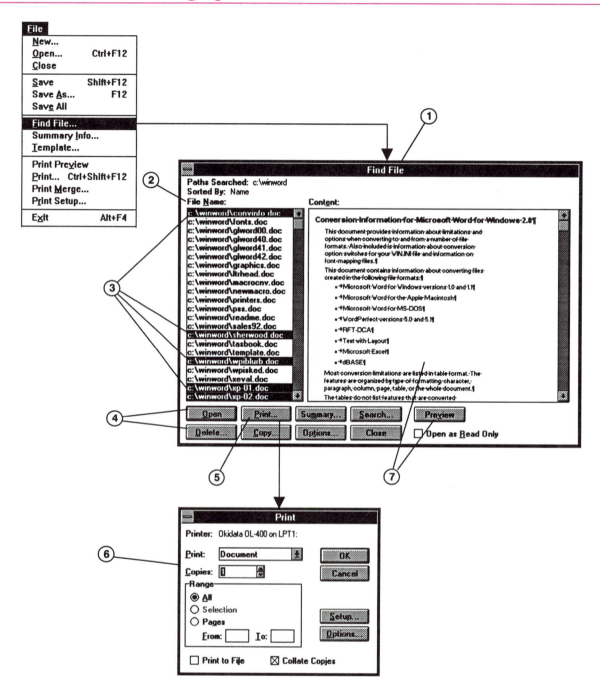

Section 42—Printing Operations—Part 2

Key	Description	Procedure or Definition
	General	The **File|Find File** menu and corresponding dialog box is used to locate and preview files. Once found, you can use the file operation buttons (item 4) to perform a variety of file operations including copying, deleting, and printing. This section shows you how to select and print multiple files. See Section 41 for more details about the **Print** dialog box (item 6).
1	Find File dialog box	Use to perform a variety of file-related operations. This dialog box lists file names and displays a view of the selected document.
2	File Name pick list	View an alphabetized list of file names here. You can select one or more files in the list.
3	Selected file names	Pick multiple files by first pressing the **Ctrl** key and then picking each file name of your choice. Deselect by picking the file name a second time.
4	Open, Delete, Copy, Summary, Options, and Search buttons	Use these buttons to process the selected file(s). Dialog boxes are displayed to guide you through most of these file operations. For example, the Delete button deletes the selected file. The Copy button prompts you for the destination and name of the copied file. Use the Summary button to display summary information about a selected document. Use the Options button to control the order in which file names are displayed. Use Search to establish file searching parameters. See Section 53 for more details.
5	Print button	Pick the Print button to display the **Print** dialog box. If you have selected two or more documents, they will be printed in alphabetical order. If you are preparing a document comprised of several different files, be sure to give each file a name that will be arranged in alphabetical order in the file name listing. For example, you may want to use names like CHAP1, CHAP2, CHAP3, etc.
6	Print dialog box	Select the print settings here. See Section 41 for details.
7	Preview button and displayed document	The Preview button is used to display a graphic representation of the document. You see the beginning of the first page and can use the scroll bars to see following pages. This is an excellent feature, because it shows you the document in addition to the file name.

Section 43—Working with Graphs—Part 1

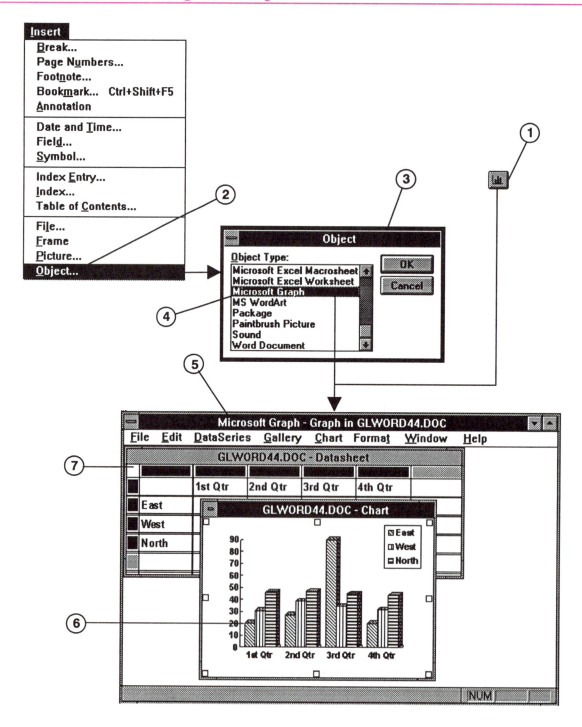

Section 43—Working with Graphs—Part 1

Key	Description	Procedure or Definition
	General	The Microsoft Graph program is included with Word. This section tells you how to access Microsoft Graph and its main parts (or *windows*). Section 44 provides information about the operation of the Microsoft Graph application. Graph is used to create a variety of graph types that are inserted into your document at the current cursor position. Once a graph is inserted, you can pick the Frame icon to put a frame around it. This lets you drag your graph to an appropriate location within your document and run text around the graph to achieve a *runaround* (see Section 25).
		Microsoft Graph is accessed using either the Graph icon (item 1) or the **Insert|Object** menu, which displays a list of objects including Microsoft Graph. When the Graph program is displayed, you can enter data values and row and column headings, select a graph type, modify colors and patterns, and add title text. Once a graph is created, return to your document using Graph's **File|Exit...** selection, or use the copy and paste keys to put the graph on a clipboard and then paste it in your document.
1	Graph icon	Pick this icon to start Microsoft Graph. If a graph already exists in a document, you can double click inside the graph to access your graph. Then you can use Microsoft Graph to make modifications.
2	Insert|Object menu	Pick the **Insert|Object** menu to display the **Object** dialog box.
3	Object dialog box	Select the *object* of your choice from the Object Type pick list and click OK to access your selection.
4	Object Type pick list	Notice that a variety of different objects are available in the **Object** dialog box pick list. To start Microsoft Graph, select it and then click OK.
5	Microsoft Graph window	The Microsoft Graph window includes a Chart window and a Datasheet window. Access either of these windows by picking them with your mouse.
6	Chart window	Use the Chart window to pick the chart type, colors, annotations, and to enter a chart title.
7	Datasheet window	Use the Datasheet window to create row and column labels and to enter data values. Once a graph is created, pick **File|Exit...** and the Yes button to return to your document. The graph is inserted at the current cursor position. Now turn to Section 44 to see more about Microsoft Graph.

Section 44—Working with Graphs—Part 2

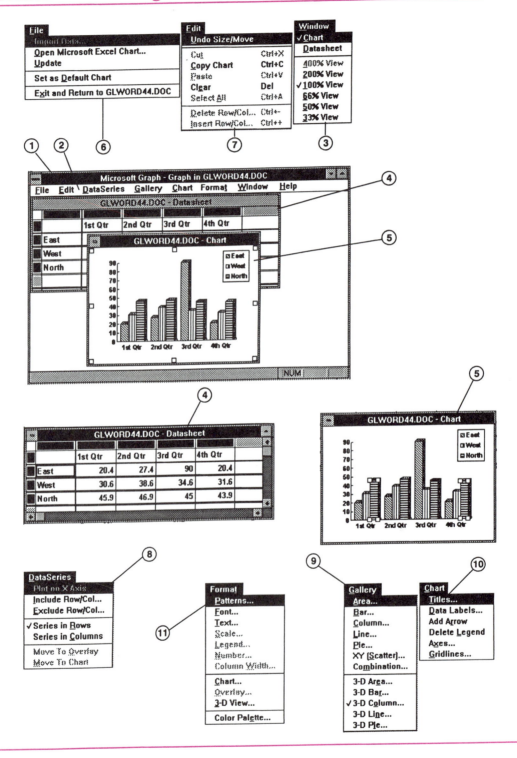

Section 44—Working with Graphs—Part 2

Key	Description	Procedure or Definition
	General	Microsoft Graph displays a Datasheet window and a Chart window. In addition, a number of menus and dialog boxes are available. Some menus apply to both the Datasheet and Chart windows, while others apply only to the Datasheet or the Chart window. This section introduces you to the operating principles behind Microsoft Graph. Experimentation with the program should clarify most of the specific features.
1	Microsoft Graph	This is the Microsoft Graph application which displays the Chart and Datasheet windows in addition to several menus.
2	Menu bar	Pick the desired menu to access the selections described in items 3, 6, 7, 8, 9, 10, and 11.
3	Window menu	Use to access and size either the Datasheet or Chart window. You can also select the window of your choice by clicking in either window.
4	Datasheet window	Use to enter row and column headings and data point values.
5	Graph window	Use to create and view the contents of your graph.
6	File menu	Use to import data or Microsoft Excel charts, update changes, reset the default Datasheet values, or to exit and return to your Word document.
7	Edit menu	Use to perform common cut, copy, paste, select, insert, delete, and undo operations.
8	DataSeries menu (use with Datasheet window)	Use to select the data to include (or exclude) as a basis for your plot and to designate either rows or columns as the primary series.
9	Gallery menu (use with Chart window)	Pick a chart type from this menu. A 3-D Column chart is shown. Each selection presents a gallery of chart styles from which to choose.
10	Chart menu (use with Chart window)	Use to add or edit titles, to insert arrows to point to data elements, to delete legends, to remove or add axis lines, and to add or remove gridlines.
11	Format menu (use with Chart and Datasheet windows)	Some selections apply to the Chart window, while others, like Number and Column width, apply to the Datasheet window. This menu lets you select or modify the patterns and colors used in the graph elements, fonts, text, scaling, legends. Use Number to select a Datasheet number format; use Column Width to set the column width used in the Datasheet.

Section 45—Working with Drawings—Part 1

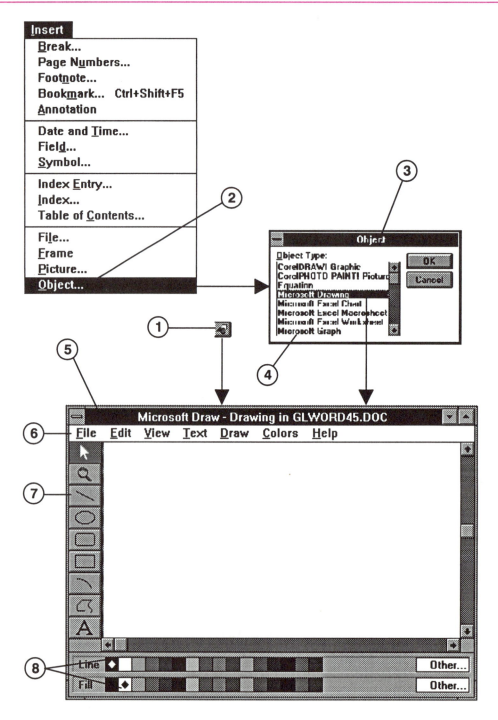

Section 45—Working with Drawings—Part 1   89

Key	Description	Procedure or Definition
	General	The Microsoft Draw program is included with Word. This is a vector graphics-oriented drawing package. Each object in the drawing is a stand-alone entity. Objects, such as lines, circles, and even passages of text can be manipulated apart from other entities within the drawing. This section tells you how to access Microsoft Draw and describes its main parts. Section 46 provides information about the operation of the Microsoft Draw program. Draw is used to create drawings or to import pictures from having formats that are compatible with the supplied filters. You can also import pictures from the clipboard. Once a drawing is ready, you can insert it in your document at the current cursor position. Then you can pick the Frame icon to put a frame around it. This lets you drag your drawing to an appropriate location within your document and run text around the drawing to achieve a *runaround* (see Section 25). Microsoft Draw is accessed using either the Draw icon (item 1) or the **Insert|Object** menu, which displays a list of objects including Microsoft Draw. When the Drawing program is displayed, you can begin drawing lines, boxes, circles, entering text, changing colors, and much more. Once a drawing is created, return to your document using Draw's **File|Exit...** selection or use the copy and paste keys to copy and paste it into your document.
1	Draw icon	Pick this icon to start Microsoft Draw. If a drawing already exists in a document, you can double click inside the drawing to access your drawing. Then you can use Microsoft Draw to make modifications.
2	Insert|Object menu	Pick the **Insert|Object** menu to display the **Object** dialog box.
3	Object dialog box	Select the *object* of your choice from the Object Type pick list and click **OK** to access your selection.
4	Object Type pick list	Notice that a variety of different objects are available in the **Object** dialog box pick list. To start Microsoft Draw, select Microsoft Drawing from the pick list and then click **OK**.
5	Microsoft Draw window	The Microsoft Draw window includes a menu bar, tools column, and color palettes. Access any of these by picking them with your mouse.
6	Menu bar	Use the menu bar to perform file, editing, view, text, drawing, and color selection operations and to display help information.
7	Drawing tools	Select a tool to add an element to your drawing.
8	Line & Fill color palettes	Use the palette to change the colors of lines and fills of the selected drawing entities.

Section 46—Working with Drawings—Part 2

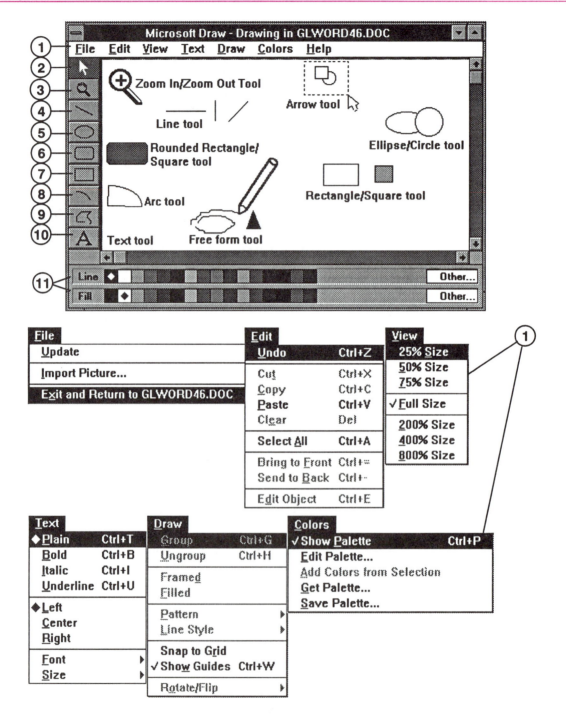

Section 46—Working with Drawings—Part 2   91

Key	*Description*	*Procedure or Definition*
	General	Microsoft Draw displays a drawing window and the necessary menus, dialog boxes, drawing tools, and color palettes to create and edit drawings that can be embedded in a document. With the exception of the **Text** menu, the menus and palettes apply to both line and text entities and are used for file handling; cutting, pasting, and copying; viewing, and coloring. Use the **Text** menu to controls the appearance of your text entities, including font selection, style, and size. This section introduces you to the operating principles behind Microsoft Draw. Experimentation with the program should reveal most of the operating techniques. The adjoining illustration provides examples of drawing entities and the Arrow, Zoom In/Out, and Free Form tool cursors.
1	Menu bar and menus	Use the menu selections to perform file operations, to change zooms, and to control the operation of line and text entities. The contents of each menu are contained in the adjoining illustration.
2	Arrow tool	Pick the Arrow tool and then an element to edit, copy, delete, or move. Select multiple elements by dragging a rubber band box around them. Selected elements display handles. Use handles to stretch or shrink.
3	Zoom In/Zoom Out tool	Pick and then place the magnifying glass icon over the element you wish to enlarge or reduce. Press **Shift** and click your mouse to reduce the view size. Perform the same operations using the **View** menu.
4	Line tool	Pick and then drag a line.
5	Ellipse/Circle tool	Pick and drag an ellipse. Press and hold **Shift** to draw a circle.
6	Rounded Rectangle/Square tool	Pick and drag a round-cornered rectangle. Press and hold **Shift** to draw a round-cornered square.
7	Rectangle/Square tool	Pick and drag a rectangle. Press and hold **Shift** to draw a square.
8	Arc tool	Pick and drag an arc. Press and hold **Shift** to draw a round circumference. Otherwise, an elliptical circumference is drawn.
9	Free Form tool	Pick and drag free-form objects. Press and release the left mouse button to draw a series of straight lines. This tool is ideal for drawing triangles and open or filled arrowheads.
10	Text tool	Pick and type your text. When handles are displayed, change fonts, sizes, and styles using the **Text** menu.
11	Line and Fill color palettes	Pick the object and pick the line or fill color from the palette. Use the **Colors** menu to modify color hues and patterns.

Section 47—Working with Equations—Part 1

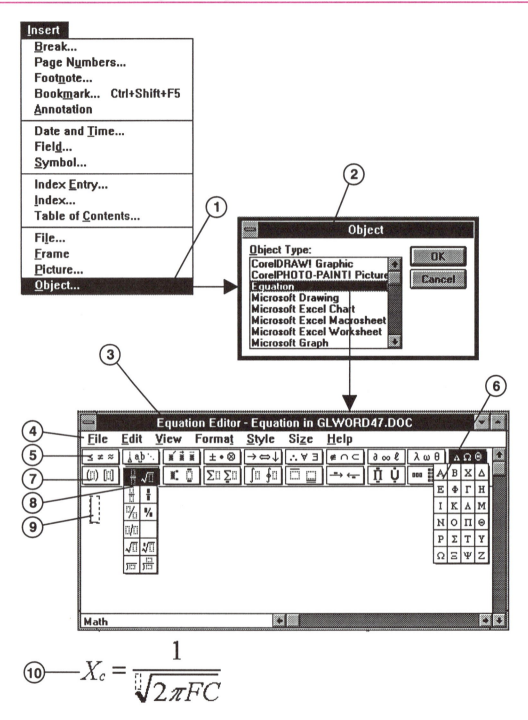

Section 47—Working with Equations—Part 1

Key	Description	Procedure or Definition
	General	The Equation Editor is a program that is supplied with Word. This program gives you the ability to put sophisticated mathematical equations into your document. It makes use of the math, Greek, and symbol fonts giving you access to the characters required to create equations. In addition, you can use the standard text fonts. Before creating an equation, you should understand the purpose of each part of the Equation Editor. In particular, you should familiarize yourself with the menus, layout templates, and special symbols and know how to *nudge* characters vertically and horizontally with **Ctrl+Arrow** keys. For example, you can nudge a subscript up (**Ctrl+Up Arrow**) to make it a superscript. Check the Equation Editor Help information to see how to insert space between characters and how to use shortcut keys. Then examine the Equation Editor menus and dialog boxes. Once an equation is created, use **File|Exit and Return** to insert the equation at the current cursor position in your document. This section provides an overview of the Equation Editor. Section 48 presents more information about the equation creation process.
1	Insert|Object menu	Pick this menu item to display the **Object** dialog box.
2	Object dialog box	Pick the Equation Editor and then click OK to start the Equation Editor program.
3	Equation Editor	Examine the Equation Editor program screen. Find the row of equation symbols (item 5) and the row of construction templates (item 7).
4	Menu bar	Use the menus to perform file, editing, viewing, and formatting operations.
5	Equation symbols	Display a symbol set of your choice by picking and holding the left mouse button.
6	Symbol pick list	Pick the desired symbol by highlighting it and releasing the mouse button. The symbol is entered into the construction template at the current cursor position.
7	Construction templates	Display a template (for a fraction, square root, etc.) by picking and holding the left mouse button.
8	Template pick list	Pick a template that satisfies your equation construction needs.
9	Entry template	Enter characters and symbols inside the displayed template.
10	Equation example	This is an example of a completed mathematical equation.

Section 48—Working with Equations—Part 2

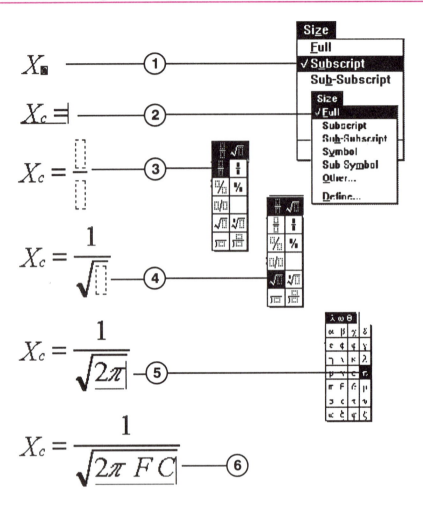

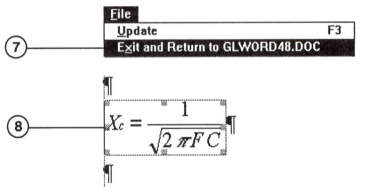

Section 48—Working with Equations—Part 2

Key	Description	Procedure or Definition
	General	This section describes the steps used to create the sample equation shown on the facing page and in Section 47. With a blank document displayed, press **Enter** twice and then move the cursor to the second line. This is the insertion point for the equation. Now start the Equation Editor by pressing **Alt+I**, pick **Object**, then select Equation, and click OK. Now perform the following procedures in items 1 through 8.
1	Full size and subscript characters	Type **Xc**, press **Shift+Left Arrow** to highlight the letter c, and pick **Subscript** from the **Size** menu.
2	Full size = sign	Pick **Full** from the **Size** menu; then type **=**.
3	Fraction template	Pick the fraction template from the second set of templates.
4	Radical (square root) template	Type **1**, press **Tab**, and pick the radical (square root) template from the second set of templates.
5	2, thin space, and pi	Type **2**, press **Shift+Spacebar** (for zero space), and insert a pi symbol by picking the pi symbol from the ninth symbol box.
6	F, C, and spaces	Press **Ctrl+Shift+Spacebar** (to insert a thick space), type **F**, press **Ctrl+Spacebar** (to insert a thin space), and type **C**. **Note:** Two thin spaces equal one thick space. To insert a 1-point space, use Ctrl+Alt+Spacebar.
7	File|Exit and Return...	Pick **Exit and Return...** from the **File** menu to insert the equation in the document at the current cursor position. Respond with **Yes** to displayed dialog box.
8	Equation in document	Check the equation in your document. Clicking inside the equation displays handles. If necessary, you can pick the Frame icon which places the equation inside a frame. Once in a frame, text can flow around the equation. You can also put a box around the equation using the **Format|Border** menu selection.

Section 49—Print Merge—Part 1

July 31, 1993

Dear :

Please read the enclosed information and respond accordingly. I'm sure you would like to share this information with your close friends in -- and invite them to join you in this exciting opportunity.

Sincerely

Ralph R. Trustworthy,
Account Representative

①

MrMs,Fname,Lname,Address,City,State,Zip

②

"Mr.","Richard","Morgan","1509 20th Street","Parkdale","CA","95092"
"Ms.","Sally","Devine","2022 Club Circle","Paxton","FL","33905"
"Dr.","Steven","Goliad","9205 Royal Lane, Suite 509","Dallas","TX","75206"
"Rev.","Thomas","Johnson","3086 21st Avenue South","St. Petersburg","FL","33038"

③

Section 49—Print Merge—Part 1

Key	Description	Procedure or Definition
	General	The Print Merge operation combines a list of information, or *data*, such as names and addresses, with a main document, such as a letter. The data can be extracted directly from a FoxPro, dBASE, or Paradox database file or from one that you type. A header document is used to identify the names of each merge field in the data file. For example, *name*, *address*, and *city* are examples of field names. Each line (or *record*) of data must include the same number of fields. Once a data and header file are created and saved, you can create a main document designed to use the information in your data file. Once typed, you use **File|Print Merge** to identify the data and header files, insert merge fields into your main document, and then perform the print merge operation. You can send the final output directly to your printer or save it to a file. A document is prepared for each line in your data file. Therefore, if you have a list of 100 names and addresses, print merge produces 100 letters. This process is ideal for sending letters to a list of friends or sales prospects. The following steps and adjoining illustration show you the documents you should create before actually performing the print merge operation. The next section steps you through the actual print merge process.
1	Main document example	Your main document can be similar to the example. Notice that no merge fields are included yet. These are inserted during the print merge operation described in the following section.
2	Header file example	Prepare and save a header file that contains a brief field name for each element in your data file. Separate each field in your data file with a comma.
3	Data file example	Create a data file similar to the example. Remember, you can specify a database file from FoxPro, dBASE, or Paradox as your data file. Be sure this is a copy of the database file, as Word converts the named file to a table. When creating your own data file, you can separate each field in your data file with a comma, although "," is preferable. If you use the "," separator, be sure to begin and end each line with a ". If you do not use quotes, Word treats commas found within data fields as field separators (or *delimiters*). Once the main document, header file, and data file are created and saved, you are ready to begin your print merge operation. Continue by turning to the next section.

Section 50—Print Merge—Part 2

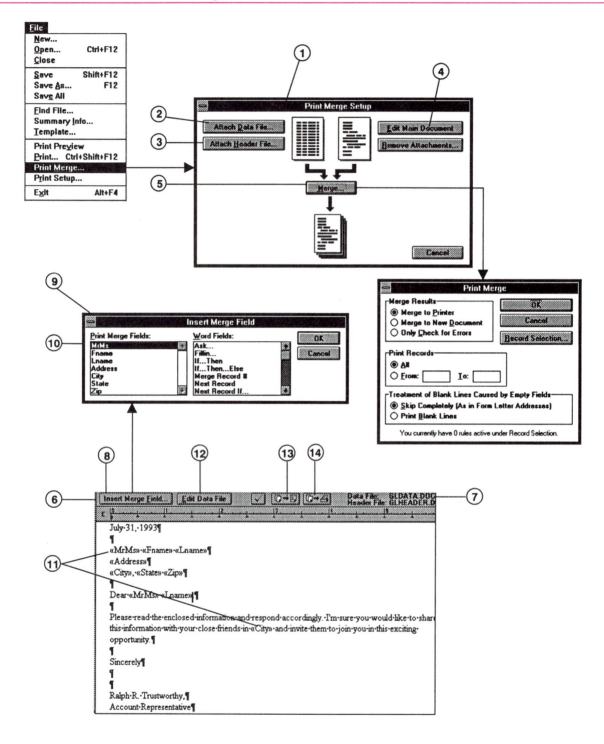

Section 50—Print Merge—Part 2

Key	Description	Procedure or Definition
	General	Prepare and save the base document, data file, and header file as described in the previous section. Then use the following procedures to complete the print merge operation.
1	Print Merge Setup dialog box	Select **File|Print Merge** to display the **Print Merge Setup** dialog box.
2	Attach Data File button	Pick this button and then supply the name of the data file.
3	Attach Header File button	Pick this button and then supply the name of the header file.
4	Edit Main Document button	Pick this button to edit the main document. This action displays it on your screen in an editing window with a special print merge toolbar.
5	Merge button	Pick to display the **Print Merge** dialog box. Use the option buttons to set up the merge operation.
6	Print merge toolbar	This special print merge toolbar displays buttons that you use to perform the print merge operation.
7	Merge file names	The names of the attached data and header files are displayed here.
8	Insert Merge Field button	Position your cursor in the main document where you want to insert a merge field. Then pick the Insert Merge Field button to access the **Insert Merge Field** dialog box.
9	Insert Merge Field dialog box	Use this dialog box to display and select your merge fields.
10	Merge field names	Pick the merge field of your choice from this list of merge field names.
11	Inserted merge fields	The merge fields are inserted into the main document at the cursor position. Be sure to type spaces and commas just as you would if you were typing the merged information. Notice that the City merge field is embedded within the body text of the main document.
12	Edit Data File button	Pick this button to edit the data file. You might want to do this if you pick the Check Mark button and discover an error, such as a missing comma, in your data file.
13	Merge to document	Pick this button to output the merged results to a file rather than to your printer.
14	Merge to printer	Pick this button to output the merged results to your printer.

100 Section 51—Fancy Type with MS WordArt—Part 1

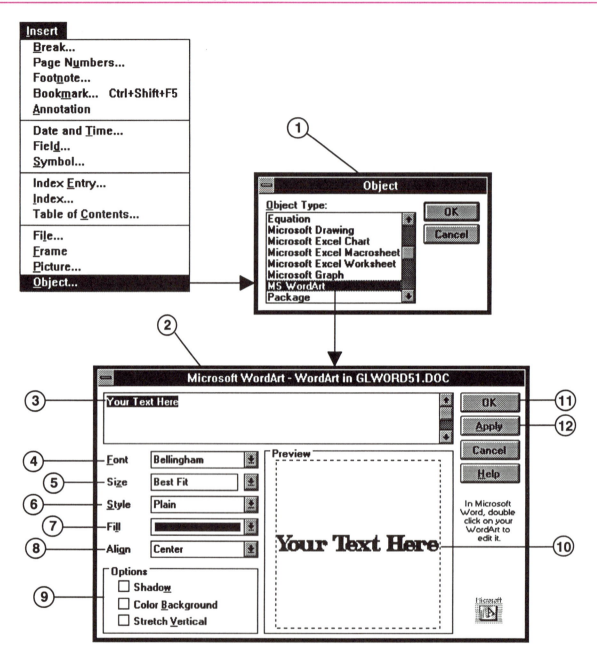

Section 51—Fancy Type with MS WordArt—Part 1   101

Key	Description	Procedure or Definition
	General	Microsoft WordArt is supplied as part of Word. WordArt is accessed through the **Insert|Object** menu. Select MS WordArt from the pick list to start the WordArt program. You can use WordArt to create and insert designer-style type into your documents. You can vary the fonts and sizes and select special effects including slanted, vertical, and arched type. You can also vary the type and background colors and add drop shadows. WordArt is ideal for creating headlines and drop capital letters. This section describes the startup procedure and identifies the parts of WordArt. The following section guides you through a hands-on activity of its use.
1	Object dialog box	Use **Insert|Object** and pick MS WordArt to start the WordArt program.
2	MS WordArt window	Enter your text and pick the font, size, style, fill, alignment, and display options. When done, click the OK button to return to your document.
3	Text entry area	Pick and type text here. End each line by pressing **Enter**. If you use the Button style, leave a blank line to prevent repetitive text.
4	Font selection box	Pick the font of your choice. Check your selections in the Preview display area.
5	Size selection box	Pick type size from the pick list or use Best Fit to fill the space allotted.
6	Style selection box	Pick Top to Bottom, Bottom to Top, Plain, Upside Down, Arch Up, Arch Down, Button, Slant Up, or Slant Down. Check your selection in the Preview display area.
7	Fill selection box	Pick the color of your choice here. If using a black and white printer, pick light shades for the best result.
8	Align selection box	Pick Left, Center, Right, Left Justify, Word Justify, or Fit Horizontally. Check your selection in the Preview display area.
9	Options check boxes	Pick one or all of the options. Check the effect of your option selections in the Preview display area.
10	Preview display	Look at the result of your selections here. Click the Apply button to see changes.
11	OK button	Pick the OK button when done. Your display type is entered into your document at the current cursor position. You may wish to put the art in a frame. To do this, pick it to display handles and then pick the Frame icon.
12	Apply button	Pick this button to see the result of your setup in the Preview display area.

102 Section 52—Fancy Type with MS WordArt—Part 2

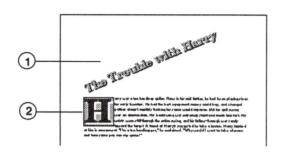

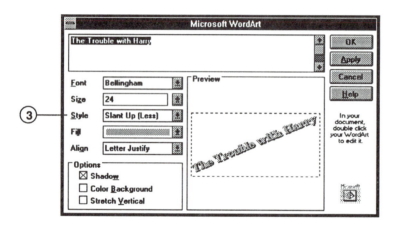

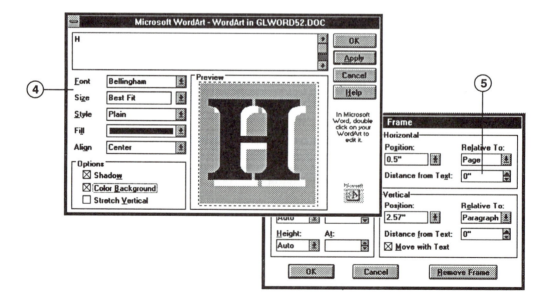

Section 52—Fancy Type with MS WordArt—Part 2

Key	Description	Procedure or Definition
	General	This section is a continuation from the previous section, which shows you how to access Microsoft WordArt and identifies the entry boxes and action buttons. This section guides you through the creation of a small document that contains two examples of WordArt. Begin on a new document. Press the **Enter** key three times and then move your cursor back to the second line. Now use **Insert|Object**, pick MS WordArt, and click **OK** to start your WordArt program.
1	Slant text example	This is an example of the slant text. The setup is given in item 3.
2	Drop capital and runaround example	This is an example of a drop capital and runaround text. Here, a frame and border are added to the WordArt and the Frame's Distance from Text is set to zero to eliminate unwanted space. The setup is given in items 4 and 5.
3	Slant text setup	a. With the cursor properly positioned, start WordArt. b. Pick inside the text entry box and type **The Trouble with Harry**. c. Set up the Font, Size, Style, Align, and Options boxes as shown. d. Click **OK** and then click **Yes** in response to the displayed prompt box. The WordArt is inserted and displayed in your document.
4	Drop capital setup	a. Position the cursor below the slanted text WordArt. b. Restart WordArt and type an **H** in the text entry box. c. Set up the Font, Size, Style, Fill, Align, and Option boxes as shown and click **OK** to insert the drop capital. d. Pick on the H to display handles. Then pick the Frame icon. e. Use **Format|Frame** and set the Distance from Text to 0" (see item 5). f. Use **Format|Border,** pick the first double line border, and pick **OK**. g. Shorten the space between the H and border lines by dragging the handles inward while pressing the **Shift** key.
5	Frame Distance from Text setup	To minimize the space between an inserted object, such as a WordArt object, graph, or picture, set the Distance from Text within the **Frame** dialog box to 0".

Section 53—Finding and Working with Files

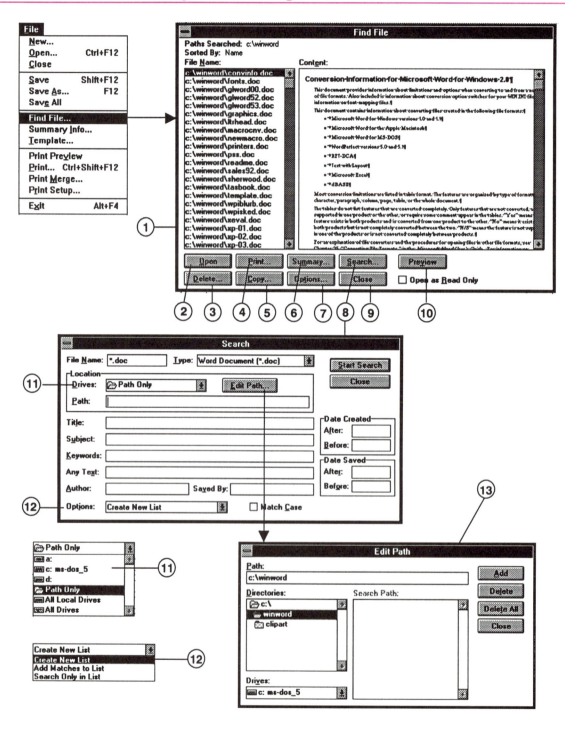

Section 53—Finding and Working with Files

Key	Description	Procedure or Definition
	General	Word's **Find File** dialog box, accessed through the **File** menu, is ideal for locating and viewing files. Once you find the file you're looking for, you can click any one of a number of action buttons used to open, copy, delete, or print selected files. You can also use the **Find File** dialog box to examine statistics about a selected file. Check the items in this table for descriptions of the operations performed with **Find File**.
1	Find File dialog box	Pick one or more files using the mouse pointer. Multiple files are selected by holding the **Shift** key down while picking the file names.
2	Open button	Click to open the selected file. This achieves the same operation as when you use Word's **File|Open** menu. The advantage to opening files from the **Find File** dialog box is that you can preview the contents first.
3	Delete button	Click to delete the selected file. You are prompted to confirm this action before the file is actually deleted.
4	Print button	Click to print one or more selected files. The **Print** dialog box is displayed prior to printing.
5	Copy button	Click to copy one or more selected files. You are prompted for a destination before selected files are copied.
6	Summary button	Click to display the **Summary Info** dialog box and file statistics.
7	Options button	Click to set Sort Files By and List File Names With options. Sorting options include Name, Author, Creation Date, Last Saved Date, etc. List File Names With options include Title, Content (preview), Summary Info, and Statistics.
8	Search button	Click to display the **Search** dialog box. Use this dialog box to set the file type, drive, and one or more paths to be searched (see items 11 through 13). You can also search by Title, Subject, Key Words, Any Text, Author, Saved By, and the creation and save dates.
9	Close button	Click to close the **Find File** dialog box.
10	Preview button	This button is displayed when the List File Names With Contents option is selected in the **Options** dialog box (see item 7).
11	Search Drives/Paths	Pick to change the drive and/or paths to be searched.
12	Search Options	Use to create a new list of file names, add matching files to the present list of file names, or to restrict searches to the current list of files.
13	Edit Path dialog box	Use this dialog box to add file paths to the search list. When one or more file paths are added to the list, use the Delete button to remove a search path. Use Delete All to clear the entire list of path names.

Section 54—Exchanging Information with Other Programs

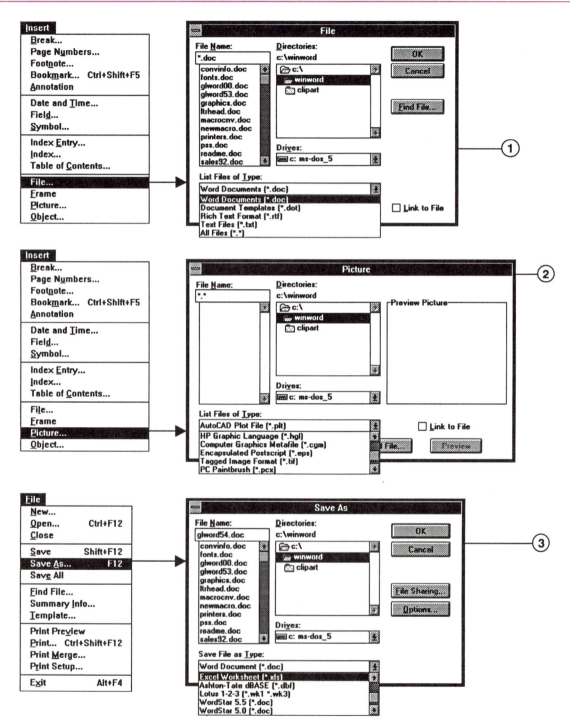

Section 54—Exchanging Information with Other Programs 107

Key	Description	Procedure or Definition
	General	Word is installed with many file *filters* that are designed to identify and convert many different kinds of files created and saved by other programs. For example, you can import files from other word processors, spreadsheets, database managers, and graphic programs. You can also export files for use by other programs by saving them with a specified format. The following items describe dialog boxes that are used to import and export files. Other Word programs, such as Microsoft Draw and Microsoft Graph, also have the ability to work with other file formats.
1	Insert|File dialog box	Use this selection to insert a file into the displayed document at the current cursor position. Use the List Files of Type pick list and select the file type of your choice. You can insert a Word for Windows file in addition to many other file types including ones created by Word for DOS, WordPerfect, WordStar, and even dBASE. For example, if you select a dBASE file with the DBF file extension, a **Convert File** dialog box is displayed. Within this dialog box is a long list of file types. Pick a valid file type and Word converts the file and inserts it into your document.
2	Insert|Picture dialog box	Use this selection to insert a picture, or *graphic file*, into your document. To specify a file type, such as PCX, use the List Files of Type pick list and select the file type of your choice. Once inserted, you can place it within a frame, making it easier to position within your text.
3	File|Save As dialog box	Use this dialog box and the Save File as Type pick list to save the current file in a format that is suitable for use with another program. In the event that a selection does not exist for the program, you may be able to save the file in an intermediate format, such as DOS Text with Layout (*.asc). Then use the other program's import feature to convert and load the saved file. This same technique is useful with graphic files. For example, you can export a file in PCX format and then import it using most of today's drawing programs.

Appendix A—Shortcut Keys

The following key sequences are used to perform a variety of word processing and display operations. The menus on the menu bar are accessed using the Alt key plus the underlined letter in the menu name. Therefore, these are not included in the list. Note that "on/off" is a *toggle*. Press once to change. Press again to change back.

Key Sequence	Description
Ctrl+Z	Undo last operation
Ctrl+X	Cut selected text or object to the clipboard
Ctrl+C	Copy selected text or object to the clipboard
Ctrl+V	Paste clipboard contents at cursor position
Ctrl+NumPad 5	Select all (entire document)
Ctrl+S	Access Style box on ribbon
Ctrl+S, Ctrl+S	Display **Style** dialog box
Ctrl+F	Access font box on ribbon
Ctrl+F, Ctrl+F	Display **Character** dialog box
Ctrl+P	Access point size box on ribbon
Ctrl+B	Boldface on/off
Ctrl+I	Italic on/off
Ctrl+U	Underline on/off
Ctrl+A	All capital letters on/off
Ctrl+D	Double underline on/off
Ctrl+H	Hidden text on/off
Ctrl+K	Small capitals on/off
Ctrl+W	Underline a word
Ctrl+Spacebar	Remove character formatting from selected text
Ctrl+L	Set text flush left
Ctrl+E	Set text centered
Ctrl+R	Set text flush right
Ctrl+J	Set text justified (flush left and right)
Ctrl+T	Set hanging indent to next tab stop
Ctrl+G	Cancel or move hanging indent to previous tab stop
Ctrl+N	Indent left margin to next tab stop
Ctrl+M	Outdent left margin to previous tab stop
Ctrl+Shift+*	Display special characters on/off (carriage returns, spaces, tabs, etc.)
Ctrl+=	Subscript on/off (3 points below baseline)
Ctrl+Shift+=	Superscript on/off (3 points above baseline)

Appendix A—Shortcut Keys

Key Sequence	Description
F1	Help
Alt+F1	Go to next field
Alt+Shift+F1	Go to the previous field
Shift+F1	Get help for a selected item
F2	Move selected text to next cursor position on **Enter**
Shift+F2	Copy selected text to next cursor position on **Enter**
Alt+F2	Display **Save As** dialog box
Alt+Shift+F2	Perform **File|Save** operation
Ctrl+F2	Increase point size by one point
Ctrl+Shift+F2	Decrease point size by one point
F3	Insert most recent glossary
Ctrl+F3	Insert text or graphics to the spike (or designation point)
Ctrl+Shift+F3	Insert/remove spike
Shift+F3	Change case of selected text
F4	Repeat last operation or typing
Ctrl+F4	Close the active document
Alt+F4	Exit current application
Shift+F4	Repeat the last find or go to command
F5	Go to page or bookmark
Alt+F5	Restore application window to its previous size
Ctrl+F5	Restore a document window to previous size
Shift+F5	Go to the previous position
Ctrl+Shift+F5	Insert a bookmark
F6	Go to the next pane
Shift+F6	Go to the previous pane
Alt+F6 or Ctrl+F6	Go to the next document window
Alt+Shift+F6 or Ctrl+Shift+F6	Go to the previous document window
F7	Check spelling of next word or selected text
Shift+F7	Display **Thesaurus** dialog box
Ctrl+F7	Move document window; then press **Enter**
Ctrl+Shift+F7	Update linked document

Appendix A—Shortcut Keys

Key Sequence	Description
F8	Extend selection to next increment (word to sentence to paragraph...)
Shift+F8	Shrink selection to previous increment
Ctrl+F8	Size a document window
Ctrl+Shift+F8	Select column (or block) mode
F9	Update a field
Alt+F9	Reduce application window to an icon
Ctrl+F9	Insert field characters
Shift+F9	Switch between showing field codes and results
Alt+Shift+F9	Replace field with previous contents; unlink field
Ctrl+Shift+F9	Replace field with last result; unlink field
F10	Activate menu bar
Alt+F10	Enlarge application window to maximum size
Ctrl+F10	Enlarge document window to maximum size
Shift+F10	Activate annotation, outline, header/footer, or button bar
Ctrl+Shift+F10	Activate ruler
F11	Go to next field
Shift+F11	Go to previous field
Ctrl+F11	Lock field
Ctrl+Shift+F11	Unlock a field
F12	Display **Save As** dialog box
Ctrl+F12	Display file **Open** dialoe box
Shift+F12	Perform **File|Save** operation
Ctrl+Shift+F12	Display **Print** dialog box

Appendix B—Field Codes

Field codes are inserted when page numbers, symbols, footnotes, annotations, index entries, table of contents entries, and other similar items are placed within your document. You can also insert field codes using **Insert|Field...**. From the **Field** dialog box, you can insert a field type by selecting one from the displayed pick list. You can also use the **Ctrl+F9** shortcut key and type the field code syntax. Field codes are displayed using **View|Field Codes**. To see a comprehensive list of field codes and their meaning, press **F1** to display help information. Then pick <u>Field Types and Instructions</u>. An overview is presented here. Read the help information about each field code type for more detailed information.

A few examples of field codes follow.

{**page** } — Page number

{**SYMBOL 190 \f"Symbol"**} — Character 190 (the em dash) of the Symbol font

{XE " examples"} — Index entry (the word "examples")

{TC "**Introduction**"} — Table of contents entry (the heading "Introduction")

{comments "Don't forget to add item 12 to this list"} — A comment to yourself; display using **View|Field Codes**

Using Ctrl+F9 When you press **Ctrl+F9**, a pair of field braces { } are inserted at the cursor position. You can type any valid field code inside the braces.

Index

About This Book, 1
Action button, 5, 33
Add button, spell check, 67
Add Line Numbering, 37
Adding Borders and Lines, 50
Align selection box, WordArt, 101
Alignment, paragraph, 31
Alignment, tab, 63
Annotation mark, 55
Annotation text, 55
Apply button, 27
Apply button, WordArt, 101
Apply To box, column, 47
Apply To button, 31
Arc tool, draw, 91
Arrow tool, draw, 91
ASCII characters, finding, 41
Attach Data File button, print merge, 99
Attach Header File button, print merge, 99
Attributes, text, 29
Auto Numbered Footnote, 55
Automating Your Work with Macros, 76
Available Formats list, date and time, 57
Available style names, 27

Backslashes, 15
Bold, 28
Boldface icon, 7
Boldfaced keys, 3
Bookmark Delete button, 59
Bookmark Name box, 59
Bookmark Name list, 59
Bookmarks (Finding Your Place), 58
Border and line examples, 50-51
Border Paragraphs dialog box, 51
Border selection, 51
Borders, adding, 50
Bullet Character, selecting, 39
Bulleted list, 39
Bulleted list icon, 6

Bullets button, 39
Button, 2

Cancel button, 13
Cancel button, grammar checks, 69
Cancel button, macro, 77
Cancel/Close button, print preview, 79
Challenged word, spelling check, 67
Change Formatting, 27
Change To suggestions, spell check, 67
Changing Document Views; Hidden Characters, 18
Character Color, 35
Character dialog box, 35
Character Font, 35
Character Map accessory, 61
Character size, points, 35
Character Spacing, 35
Character Style, 35
Chart menu, graph, 87
Chart window, graph, 85
Check box, 2
Clear button, find, 41
Click, 3
Close (file), 11
Close button, Find File, 105
Closing Files, 12
Collate Copies check box, 81
Color, character, 35
Color, border, 51
Column adjust cursor, table, 45
Column icon, 7
Column icon, 47
Column Width, table, 43, 45
Columnar text examples, 46-47
Columns, working with, 46
Comments box, 15
Completion dialog box, spell check 67
Confirm check box, hyphenation, 73
Construction templates, equations, 93
Cont. Notice button, footnote, 55

Cont. Separator button, footnote, 55
Convention Used In This Book, 3
Converted table example, 32
Copied and pasted text, 23
Copies, print, 81
Copy button, Find File, 105
Copy icon, 6
Current page number, 12
Current section number, 37
Current style name, 27
Cursor, text, 17
Cursor, column adjust, table, 45
Cursor control keys, 17
Custom Footnote Mark, 55
Custom zoom value, 19
Cut text, 23

Data file, print merge, 97
DataSeries menu, graph, 87
Datasheet window, graph, 85, 87
Date example, 56-57
Dates, 57
Default, 2
Default tab stop, 9, 33
Define button, 27
Define Style, 27
Delete button, macro, 77
Delete button, Find File, 105
Delete Cells/Rows/ or Columns, 45
Delete character or word, 21
Delete to the beginning of the current line, 21
Delete to the end of the current line, 21
Deleted text, 25
Deleting a graphic, 21
Description, 27
Description box, macro, 77
Diagonal cursor, 49
Dialog box, 2, 4-5
Different First Page, headers and footers, 53
Different Odd and Even Pages, headers and footers, 53

Index

Different styles shown, 27
Directories box, 11, 15
Disk drive designator, 15
Diskette icon, 6
Display, 1
Distance From Edge, headers and footers, 53
Distance from Text, frame, 49
Document options check boxes, print, 81
Dot leader example, 62-63
Dot Leaders, 62
Drag, 3
Drag left/right, 17
Drag up/down, 17
Draw icon, 7, 89
Drawing tools, 89
Drawings, Working with, 88-91
Drives box, 15
Drives selection box, 11
Drop capital, WordArt, 103

Edit button, macro, 77
Edit Data File button, print merge, 99
Edit Main Document button, print merge, 99
Edit menu, graph, 87
Edit Path dialog box, Find File, 105
Edit|Find, 41
Edit|Replace, 41
Ellipse/Circle tool, draw, 91
Ellipsis, 2
Em dash, 60
Entry template, equations, 93
Envelope, print, 7
Envelope icon, 7
Envelope options check box, print, 81
Equation editor, 93
Equation example, 92-93
Equation in document example, 94-95
Equation symbols, 93
Equations, Working with, 92-95

Eraser icon, 6
Even # page header, 53
Exchanging Information with Other Programs, 106
Explain button, grammar checks, 69
Export files, 107

Facing pages, 31
Fancy Type with MS WordArt, 100-103
Field Code box, 57
Field codes, 113
File, close, 11
File, find, 11
File, new, 11
File, open, 11
File, save, 11
File, Save As, 11
File Exit and Return, equations, 95
File export, 107
File extension, 15
File filters, 107
File folder icon, 6
File import, 107
File menu, graph, 87
File name, 15
File Name box, 11, 15
File Name pick list, 15
File Name pick list, print, 83
File path box, 11
File Sharing button, 15
File|Close, 13
File|Save As dialog box, 107
Fill selection box, WordArt, 101
Filters, file, 107
Find and Replace, 40
Find dialog box, 41
Find Direction buttons, 41
Find File, 11
Find File buttons, 83
Find File dialog box, print, 83
Find File dialog box, 105
Find Formatting buttons, 41
Find Next button, 41

Find What box, 41
Finding and Working with Files, 105
Finding ASCII characters, 41
Flush right tab on ruler, 63
Font box, 7
Font box pick list, 7
Font examples, 29
Font name box, 29
Font name pick list, 29
Font selection box, WordArt, 101
Fonts, Type Sizes, and Text Attributes, 28
Footer, 53
Footnote mark, 55
Footnote Options button, 55
Footnote text, 55
Footnotes and Annotations, 54
Format menu, 35
Format menu, graph, 87
Format|Border Table dialog box, 43
Format|Columns dialog box, 47
Format|Frame dialog box, 49
Format|Section Layout, 37
Format|Style menu, 27
Format Text (Sections), 36
Formatting Text (Pages, Paragraphs, and Characters), 34, 36
Fraction template, equations, 95
Frame "handles", 49
Frame cursor, 49
Frame Distance from Text, WordArt example, 103
Frame example, 48-49
Frame icon, 7, 49
Free Form tool, draw, 91
From Text, border, 51
Full size characters, equations, 95

Gallery menu, graph, 87
Go To (F5), 17
Go To entry area, 59
Grammar Checks, 68
Grammar dialog box, 69
Graph icon, 7, 85

Index 117

Graph window, 87
Graphical reference, 1
Graphs, Working with, 84-87
Gridlines, table, 43
Gutter, 31

Hanging Indent, 31
Hanging Indent By, 39
Hanging Indent By, bullets, 39
Hardware Requirements, 1
Header, 53
Header file, print merge, 97
Header/Footer dialog box, 53
Headers and Footers, 52
Heading separator buttons, index, 65
Height cursor, 49
Help button, 13
Hidden characters, 18
Highlight, 3
Horizontal Position, frame, 49
Horizontal scroll bar, 9
Hot Zone, hyphenation, 73
How To Use This Book, 1
Hyphenate At box, 73
Hyphenate CAPS check box, 73
Hyphenation, Using, 72
Hyphenation dialog box, 73

Icon, 2
Ignore and Ignore All buttons, spell check, 67
Ignore button, grammar checks, 69
Import files, 107
Include options check boxes, print, 81
Increase/decrease selector, 5
Indent First Line, 31
Indent From Left, 31
Indent From Left & Right, 31
Indent From Right, 31
Indent icon, 6
Index dialog box, 65
Index Entry dialog box, 65
Index Entry text box, 65

Index example, 64-65
Indexes and Tables of Contents, 64
Insert buttons, index, 65
Insert Cells/Rows/ or Columns, 45
Insert Field Type list, 57
Insert File dialog box, 107
Insert Merge Field button, 99
Insert Picture dialog box, 107
Insert Table dialog box, 43
Insert/strikeover mode, 21
Insert|Bookmark, 59
Insert|Date and Time, 57
Insert|Field dialog box, 113
Insert|Field menu, 57
Insert|Footnote dialog box, 55
Insert|Object menu, draw, 89
Insert|Object menu, equations, 93
Insert|Object menu, graph, 85
Insert|Page Numbers, 57
Inserting and Deleting Text, 20
Inserting Special Characters and Symbols, 60
Insertion point (cursor), 21
Instructions list, field, 57
Italic, 28
Italic icon, 7

Key assignment, 5
Keystroke, 2
Keywords/Comments box, 15

Landscape, 31
Leaders, 33
Leader, tab, 63
Line & Fill color palettes, draw, 89
Line and column no., 9
Line and Fill color palettes, draw, 91
Line Between check box, columns, 47
Line examples, 50-51
Line Number format and placement, 37
Line Numbers button, 37
Line Spacing, 31

Line tool, draw, 91
Lines, adding, 50
Lines selection, border, 51
List Files of Type box, 11
Long dash symbol, 61
Look Up button, thesaurus, 71

Macro dialog box, 77
Macro Name box, 77
Macro text example, 76-77
Macros, 76
Main document, print merge, 97
Margin setting, 31
Margin value boxes, 31
Margins, Indents, Outdents, and Line Spacing, 30
Margins, 35
Margins button, print preview, 79
Match Case check box, 41
Match Whole Word Only check box, 41
Meanings List, thesaurus, 71
Memory, 1
Menu, 2
Menu bar, 2, 5
Menu bar, draw, 89
Menu bar, equations, 93
Menu bar, graph, 87
Menu bar and menus, draw, 91
Menu name, 5
Menu selection, 5
Menus and Dialog boxes, 4
Merge button, print merge, 99
Merge Cells, table, 45
Merge field names, 99
Merge file names, print merge, 99
Merge to file (or document), 99
Merge to printer button, 99
Microsoft Draw window, 89
Microsoft Graph window, 85, 87
Mouse pointer, 2
Move with Text check box, frame, 49
Moving Around in a Document, 16

MS-DOS, 1

Naming documents, 14-15
New (file), 11
New document icon, 6
Next page, 17
Next page icon, 9
No button, 13
None/Custom buttons, border, 51
Normal ruler, 33
Normal text, 31
Num Lock status, 9
Number Format, 39
Number Format, headers and footers, 53
Number Format, page, 57
Number of Columns, 47
Number Separator, 39
Number Start At, 39
Numbered and Bulleted Lists, 38
Numbered list, 39
Numbered List button, 39
Numbered list icon, 6
Numbering Start At, footnote, 55

Object dialog box, graph, 85
Object dialog box, equations, 93
Object dialog box, WordArt, 101
Object Type pick list, draw, 89
Object Type pick list, graph, 85
Odd # page header, 53
One Page or Two Pages button, print preview, 79
Open (file), 11
Open button, Find File, 105
Opening files, 10
Opening Multiple Documents with the Window Menu, 74
Option buttons, 5
Options button, 2
Options button, Find File, 105
Options button, grammar checks, 69
Options button, spell check, 67
Options check boxes, WordArt, 101

Options dialog box, grammar checks, 69
Options dialog box, print, 81
Orientation, page, 31, 35
Outdent, 31
Outdent icon, 6

Page # fields, headers and footers, 53
Page display icons, 7
Page No. Alignment, 57
Page No. Format, 57
Page No. Position, 57
Page Number, index entry, 65
Page number example, 56-57
Page Number Format dialog box, headers and footers, 53
Page number(s), print preview, 79
Page number/total number of pages, 12
Page Numbering, 57
Page Numbering, headers and footers, 53
Page Numbers and Dates, 56
Page Setup dialog box, 35
Page size & orientation, 31
Page width icon, 19
Paragraph Alignment, 31, 35
Paragraph dialog box, 35
Paragraph icon, 7
Paragraph Indentation, 31, 35
Paragraph Line Spacing, 35
Paragraph Pagination, 31, 35
Paragraph Spacing, 31, 35
Paste icon, 6
Path (or directory) name, 15
Pick, 3
Place At, footnote, 55
Point Size, bullets, 39
Point size box, 29
Point size pick list, 29
Points (character size), 35
Portrait, page orientation, 31
Preset (border type), 51

Preview button, Find File, 105
Preview button and displayed document, 82-83
Preview display, WordArt, 101
Previous page, 17
Previous page icon, 9
Print button, 79
Print button, Find File, 83, 105
Print dialog box, 81, 83
Print document name, 81
Print icon, 81
Print Merge, 96-99
Print merge example, 99
Print Merge Setup dialog box, 99
Print merge toolbar, 99
Print multiple files, 83
Print Preview, 78
Print Preview display, 79
Print Setup dialog box, 81
Print to File check box, 81
Printer, 81
Printer icon, 7
Printing Operations, 80-83
Printing options check boxes, 81

Radical (square root) template, equations, 95
Range options, print, 81
Readability Statistics, grammar checks, 69
Record Macro dialog box, 77
Record macro Name box, 77
Rectangle/Square tool, draw, 91
Remove button, bullets, 39
Remove button, numbered and bulleted lists, 39
Remove Frame button, 49
Rename button, macro, 77
Repeat and undo operations, 24
Repeat Edit Clear, 25
Repeat Typing, 25
Repeated text, 25
Repeating Text, 25
Replace All button, 41

Index 119

Replace button, 41
Replace button, thesaurus, 71
Replace dialog box, 41
Replace Only Bullets, 39
Replace Only Numbers, numbered lists, 39
Replace With box, 41
Replace With box, thesaurus, 71
Restart at (line numbers), 37
Ribbon, 2, 6
Rounded rectangle/Square took, draw, 91
Row Height, table, 45
Ruled table example, 42
Ruler, Scroll Bars, and Status Line, 8
Ruler, 9
Ruler scale, 9
Run button, macro, 77
Runarounds, 48

Save (file), 11
Save As, file, 11
Save File as Type box, 15
Saving and Naming Documents, 14
Scroll bar, 2, 9
Scroll button, 9
Scroll down, 17
Scroll down arrow, 9
Scroll left arrow, 11
Scroll right arrow, 9
Scroll right/left, 17
Scroll up, 17
Scroll up arrow, 9
Search button, Find File, 105
Search Drives/Paths, Find File, 105
Search Options, Find File, 105
Section examples, 36-37
Section Layout dialog box, 37
Section number, 12
Section Start, 37
Select, 3
Select Row, table, 45
Selected file names, print, 83
Selected text, 23

Selected word in text, thesaurus, 71
Selected word in text, hyphenation, 73
Selecting, Cutting, Pasting, and Copying, 22
Selection box, 5
Sentence, grammar checks, 69
Separator button, footnote, 55
Set button, tabs, 63
Setting Tabs, 32
Setup dialog box, print, 81
Shading dialog box, border, 51
Shortcut key, 5
Shortcut Key box, 27
Shortcut Keys, 109-111
Shortcut Key, macro, 77
Show buttons, macro, 77
Size, frame, 49
Size and Orientation, page, 35
Size selection box, WordArt, 101
Slant text, WordArt, 103
Software Requirements, 1
Space Between, columns, 47
Spaces, equations, 95
Spacing, paragraph, 31
Spacing, Line, 31
Special cursor control keys, 17
Special Find Characters, 41
Spell check icon, 7
Spelling Checks, 66
Spelling dialog box, 67
Split Table, 45
Start New Column check box, 47
Statistics button, 15
Status line, 9
Style box, 7
Style buttons, 27
Style dialog box, 27
Style Name box, 27
Style selection box, WordArt, 101
Subdirectory (or file path) box, 11
Subject box, 15
Subscript characters, equations, 95
Suggest button, spell check, 67

Suggestions, grammar checks, 69
Summary button, Find File, 105
Superscript/Subscript, 35
Symbol examples, 60-61
Symbol pick list, equation, 93
Symbols dialog box, 61
Symbols From box and pick list, 61
Synonyms For box, thesaurus, 71
Synonyms pick list, thesaurus, 71

Tab Alignment, 33
Tab icons (on ribbon), 33
Tab stop, default, 33
Tab stop example, 32
Tab Stop Position, 33, 63
Tab style icons, 7, 9
Tabbed text example, 32
Table Creation, 42
Table example, 44
Table icon, 7, 43
Table of Contents dialog box, 65
Table tabs, 33
Table|Convert Text to Table, 43
Table|Select Table, 43
Tables, working with, 42-45
Tables of contents, 64
Tabs, setting, 32
Tabs dialog box, 33, 63
Template pick list, equations, 93
Terms, Definitions, and Conventions, 2
Text alignment icons, 7
Text attribute icons, 29
Text box, 2, 5
Text cursor, 17
Text entry area, WordArt, 101
Text tool, draw, 91
Text Wrapping, frame, 49
Thesaurus, Using the, 70
Thesaurus dialog box, 71
Title box, 15
Toolbar, 2, 6
Tools|Bullets and Numbering dialog box, 39

Tools|Stop Recorder, 77
Type size icon, 7
Type size pick list, 7

Underline, 28
Underline icon, 7
Undo and Repeat Operations, 24
Undo Edit Clear, 25
Undo Last button, spell check, 67
Undo Typing, 25
Use Heading Paragraphs button, table of contents, 65
Use Table Entry Fields button, table of contents, 65

Vertical Alignment, 37
Vertical position, 9
Vertical Position, frame, 49
Vertical scroll bar, 9

Vertical scroll button, 9
View|Annotations, 55
View|Draft, 19
View|Field Codes, 19
View|Footnotes, 55
View|Normal, 19
View|Outline, 19
View|Page Layout, 19
View|Ribbon, 19
View|Ruler, 19
View|Toolbar, 19
View|Zoom, 19

What You Should Know, 1
Whole page icon, 19
Width cursor, 49
Window menu, graph, 87
Window|1, 2, ..., 75
Window|Arrange All, 75

Window|New Window, 75
Windows, 1
Wingdings symbols, 61
WordArt examples, 102-103
WordArt window, 101
Working with Frames; Runarounds, 48
Working with Styles, 26

Yes button, 13

Zoom, Custom, 19
Zoom 100% icon, 19
Zoom In/Zoom Out tool, draw, 91
Zoom percentage, 9
Zoom to page width, 19
Zoom to whole page, 19
Zoom|Magnifications, 19

Computer Aided Drafting
Illustrated AutoCAD (Release 11)
Illustrated AutoCAD (Release 12)
Illustrated AutoLISP
Illustrated AutoSketch 2.0
Illustrated Generic CADD Level 3

Database Management
Illustrated dBASE III Plus
Illustrated dBASE IV 1.1
Illustrated Force 2
Illustrated FoxPro 2.0

Desktop Publishing
The Desktop Studio: Multimedia with the Amiga
Illustrated PFS:First Publisher 2.0 & 3.0
Illustrated PageMaker 4.0
Illustrated Ventura 3.0 (Windows Ed.)
Illustrated Ventura 3.0 (DOS/GEM Ed.)
Illustrated Ventura 4.0

General and Advanced Topics
111 Clipper Functions
The Complete Communications Handbook
Financial Modeling using Lotus 1-2-3
Graphic User Interface Programming with C
Illustrated DacEasy Accounting 4.2
Illustrated Novell NetWare 2.x/3.x Software
Integrating TCP/IP into SNA
Learn P-CAD Master Designer 6.0
Novell NetWare: Adv. Tech. and App.
Programming On-Line Help with Turbo C/C++
Understanding 3COM Networks

Integrated
Illustrated Enable/OA
Illustrated Framework III
Illustrated Microsoft Works 2.0
Illustrated Q&A 3.0 (2nd Ed.)
Illustrated Q&A 4.0

Programming Languages
Illustrated Borland C++ 3.1
Illustrated C Programming (ANSI) (2nd Ed.)
Illustrated Clipper 5.0 (2nd Ed.)
Illustrated QBasic for MS-DOS 5.0
Graphics Programming with Turbo Pascal
Illustrated Turbo C++
Illustrated Turbo Debugger 3.0
Illustrated Turbo Pascal 6.0

Spreadsheet
Illustrated Excel 4.0 for Windows
Illustrated Lotus 1-2-3 Rel. 2.2
Illustrated Lotus 1-2-3 Rel. 3.0
Illustrated Quattro

Systems and Operating Guides
Illustrated DR DOS 6.0
Illustrated MS-DOS 5.0
Illustrated UNIX System V
Illustrated Windows 3.1

Word Processing
Illustrated Microsoft Word 5.0 (PC)
Illustrated WordPerfect 1.0 (Macintosh)
Illustrated WordPerfect 5.1
Illustrated WordPerfect for Windows
Illustrated WordStar 6.0
WordPerfect Wizardry: Advanced Techniques and Applications

Call Wordware Publishing, Inc. for names of the bookstores in your area
(214) 423-0090

Popular Applications Series
Build Your Own Computer
Cost Control Using Lotus 1-2-3
Creating Newsletters with Ventura
Database Publishing with Ventura
Desktop Pub. with Word 2.0 for Windows
Desktop Pub. with WordPerfect for Windows
Learn AmiPro 3.0 in a Day
Learn AutoCAD in a Day
Learn AutoCAD 12 in a Day
Learn C in Three Days
Learn CorelDRAW! in a Day
Learn DataPerfect in a Day
Learn dBASE Programming in a Day
Learn DOS in a Day
Learn DrawPerfect in a Day
Learn Excel for Windows in a Day (Ver. 3.0/4.0)
Learn FoxPro 2.0 in a Day
Learn Freelance Graphics for Windows in a Day
Learn Generic CADD 6.0 in a Day
Learn Harvard Graphics 3.0 in a Day
Learn Lotus 1-2-3 Ver. 2.4 in a Day
Learn Microsoft Assembler in a Day
Learn Microsoft Works in a Day
Learn Norton Utilities in a Day
Learn Novell NetWare Software in a Day
Learn OS/2 in a Day
Learn Pacioli 2000 Ver. 2.0 in a Day
Learn PageMaker 4.0 in a Day
Learn PAL in a Day
Learn Paradox 4.0 in a Day
Learn Paradox for Windows in a Day
Learn Pascal in Three Days
Learn PC-Paintbrush in a Day
Learn PC-Tools 8.0 in a Day

Popular Applications Series Cont.
Learn PlanPerfect in a Day
Learn Q&A in a Day
Learn Quattro Pro 4.0 in a Day
Learn Quicken in a Day
Learn Turbo Assembler Prog. in a Day
Learn Ventura 4.0 in a Day
Learn Windows in a Day
Learn Windows NT in a Day
Learn Word 2.0 for Windows in a Day
Learn WordPerfect 5.2 for Windows in a Day
Learn WordPerfect in a Day (2nd Edition)
Mailing Lists using dBASE
Moving from WordPerfect for DOS to
 WordPerfect for Windows
Object-Oriented Prog. using Turbo C++
Presentations with Harvard Graphics
Programming Output Drivers using
 Borland C++
WordPerfect Macros
WordPerfect 6.0 Survival Skills
Write Your Own Programming Language
 using C++

At A Glance Series
FoxPro 2.5 at a Glance
FoxPro for Windows at a Glance
Lotus 1-2-3 for Windows at a Glance
Microsoft Windows at a Glance
Paradox for Windows at a Glance
Quattro Pro 4.0 at a Glance
Quattro Pro for Windows at a Glance
Word 2.0 for Windows at a Glance
WordPerfect 5.2 for Windows at a Glance

100 Days in Texas: The Alamo Letters
by Wallace O. Chariton

Classic Clint: The Laughs and Times of Clint Murchison, Jr.
by Dick Hitt

Country Savvy: Survival Tips for Farmers, Ranchers, and Cowboys
by Reed Blackmon

Critter Chronicles
by Jim Dunlap

Dirty Dining: A Cookbook, and More, for Lovers
by Ginnie Siena Bivona

Don't Throw Feathers at Chickens: A Collection of Texas Political Humor
by Charles Herring, Jr. and Walter Richter

Exploring the Alamo Legends
by Wallace O. Chariton

From an Outhouse to the Whitehouse
by Wallace O. Chariton

The Great Texas Airship Mystery
by Wallace O. Chariton

Kingmakers
by John R. Knaggs

Rainy Days in Texas Funbook
by Wallace O. Chariton

Recovery: A Directory to Texas Substance Abuse Treatment Facilities
Edited by Linda Manning-Miller

San Antonio Uncovered
by Mark Louis Rybczyk

Spirits of San Antonio and South Texas
by Docia Schultz Williams and Reneta Byrne

Texas Highway Humor
by Wallace O. Chariton

Texas Politics in My Rearview Mirror
Waggoner Carr and Byron Varner

Texas Tales Your Teacher Never Told You
by Charles F. Eckhardt

Texas Wit and Wisdom
by Wallace O. Chariton

That Cat Won't Flush
by Wallace O. Chariton

That Old Overland Stagecoaching
by Eva Jolene Boyd

They Don't Have to Die
by Jim Dunlap

This Dog'll Hunt
by Wallace O. Chariton

To The Tyrants Never Yield
by Kevin R. Young

A Trail Rider's Guide to Texas
by Mary Elizabeth Sue Goldman

Unsolved Texas Mysteries
by Wallace O. Chariton

Call Wordware Publishing, Inc. for names of the bookstores in your area
(214) 423-0090